Relief Carving with
Nora Hall

Schiffer Publishing Ltd

4880 Lower Valley Road Atglen, Pennsylvania 19310

Dedicated to Han Leereveld, my Father

You're not with us anymore, Pap, but I wish you were here to look through this book that I dedicated to you. How surprised and happy you would be to see our carving methods being passed on and used. Pap, I'm teaching the same ones that go way back for generations, the ones you learned from your boss when you were an apprentice and the ones you taught me. Wish you were here, Pap!

Other Schiffer Books on Related Subjects:
Relief Carving with Bob Lundy. Bob Lundy. ISBN: 0887404391. $14.95
Scenic Relief Carving. Georg Keilhofer. ISBN: 0887407889. $12.95

Copyright © 2011 by Nora Hall

Library of Congress Control Number: 2011935630

All rights reserved. No part of this work may be reproduced or used in any form or by any means—graphic, electronic, or mechanical, including photocopying or information storage and retrieval systems—without written permission from the publisher.

The scanning, uploading and distribution of this book or any part thereof via the Internet or via any other means without the permission of the publisher is illegal and punishable by law. Please purchase only authorized editions and do not participate in or encourage the electronic piracy of copyrighted materials.

"Schiffer," "Schiffer Publishing Ltd. & Design," and the "Design of pen and inkwell" are registered trademarks of Schiffer Publishing Ltd.

Cover and book designed by: Bruce Waters
Type set in Zurich Blk BT/Zurich BT

ISBN: 978-0-7643-3938-7
Printed in China

Schiffer Books are available at special discounts for bulk purchases for sales promotions or premiums. Special editions, including personalized covers, corporate imprints, and excerpts can be created in large quantities for special needs. For more information contact the publisher:

Published by Schiffer Publishing Ltd.
4880 Lower Valley Road
Atglen, PA 19310
Phone: (610) 593-1777; Fax: (610) 593-2002
E-mail: Info@schifferbooks.com

For the largest selection of fine reference books on this and related subjects, please visit our website at **www.schifferbooks.com**
We are always looking for people to write books on new and related subjects. If you have an idea for a book, please contact us at proposals@schifferbooks.com

This book may be purchased from the publisher.
Include $5.00 for shipping.
Please try your bookstore first.
You may write for a free catalog.

In Europe, Schiffer books are distributed by
Bushwood Books
6 Marksbury Ave.
Kew Gardens
Surrey TW9 4JF England
Phone: 44 (0) 20 8392 8585; Fax: 44 (0) 20 8392 9876
E-mail: info@bushwoodbooks.co.uk
Website: www.bushwoodbooks.co.uk

Contents

Acknowledgements 4
Foreword 5
Introduction 6
Chapter 1 My Life as a Woodcarver 8
Chapter 2 The German Occupation 12
Chapter 3 The Methods of the Masters 16
Chapter 4 Seventeenth Century Dutch Panel 19
    Exercise 1 - Ribbon 20
    Exercise 2 - Ribbon 23
Chapter 5 Letter Carving 42
    The V Tool 43
    Letter L 45
    Letter J 49
    Letters B & S 66
Chapter 6 Carving the Crest 75
    Pearls and Shells 76
    Lily Leaves 79
    Top Scrolls 81
    Bottom Scrolls 83
    Step by Step 85
Chapter 7 Some Passing Thoughts 105
Appendix A Tool Shape Identification 106
Appendix B Nora Hall's "How To Carve" Videos and Tools 107
Nora Hall's Sample Portfolio 107

Acknowledgments

Like many authors, it was not my original intent to write a book at all. It was the repeated encouragement of others that finally convinced me to put my thoughts together and organize them into a publication to be shared, so others can learn what I know about woodcarving. In other words, when people began to realize my effective carving method and the passion I had to teach it, they became very insistent that I preserve my knowledge in the form of a manuscript.

Some of those people actually contributed to the book and, for that reason, deserve recognition. I feel like I have a support group of very talented people who had blind faith in me and the concepts I had already produced for this book. I will now list them, but I want the reader to know, they are not presented in order of importance for each was equally valuable in his or her own way. This was a team effort. I say, "Thank you," to all of them. This is your book as much as it is mine.

Tom Krent photographed all of the current carving projects and rejuvenated images of earlier works that were captured on film.

Charles Rogers is one of those friends that everybody would like to have. His woodcarving skills and knowledge, combined with a mastery of the spoken and written English language, resulted in hours of deep conversations in which he provided priceless input for the book.

My daughter, Renée Mestan, is the best public relations person an artist could have. Lucky me! She is tireless and passionate about getting the message out that (in her words) her mom is the best carver, teacher, and person in general in the world. As you might imagine, her enthusiasm has to be tempered a bit sometimes, but that's OK.

My son, Swen Nater, has everything a mother admires and more. He is an accomplished author himself, with several published books. He was a tremendous help in giving the book a more professional shape as he revised much of what I wrote down.

Tom's wife, Terry Matheys-Krent, spent hours going through all of my writings and editing with great enthusiasm. Thank you, Terry.

Reana Mestan, my granddaughter, did lots of typing for the projects. She was always ready for the job. I love you, Reana.

I can see my late husband, Sam, smiling in the background. He loved me, and no matter what undertaking I tackled, he supported me and believed in me. He had much to do with this adventure. Thank you for everything, Sam. Thank you for just being you.

Last, but not least, thanks go to my son, Wendell Langeberg, a carver himself. Wendell put his professional touches to the book and provided the patterns in the book. He will no doubt continue the carving legacy in our family.

Foreword

Most artisans, even a renown hands-on teacher like Nora Hall, cannot reach the wide audience their gifts demand by small class instruction. Consequently, they rely on a variety of media. Nora has constantly traveled around the country teaching classes and, for many years, has offered demonstration videos and plaster casts as teaching aids. This book is another effort to promote the art of woodcarving through an explanation of her techniques. Amateurs and professionals alike should welcome another book into their growing woodcarving library.

This book is part autobiography and part step-by-step instruction without the academic and, frankly, tiresome iteration of materials and equipment so prevalent in most books on the craft. There is a refreshing directness here, which only a seasoned teacher can have.

The freedom of expression Nora emphasizes by her method serves to allow students to make their own subtle decisions regarding the details of the shape, to build confidence within the framework of an overall design. Though the range of projects explained seems to be limited, Nora has chosen ones which have many challenges and a number of perceptual problems to solve. With mastery of these exercises, the student achieves an admirable level of competence. The gifted teacher is most effective when serving primarily as a guide, and, in a manual art such as woodcarving, wisdom leaves it there.

Frederick Wilbur

Introduction

I wrote this book because I want you to experience the pure joy that I, and many others, experience when time seems to stand still as we create beautiful art with our own two hands. Wood is beautiful and has many characteristics that only this natural material can have. However, I will be happy if I can just spark your interest in this unique art form of woodcarving. The free expression of your natural, artistic side will give you a feeling of total satisfaction and enjoyment that you may not get from any other form of art.

There is a lot of knowledge passed down through the generations that has disappeared from books today. What has disappeared? Things like how to carve easily and with more speed, using fewer tools, and how to remove the wood. Things that were taught from an old world master to his apprentice. I realize that the old masters are all but gone, but I feel that I must pass on this very valuable information before the knowledge is lost to time.

I will address mostly high and low relief carving; however, this information can be applied to all types of carving. Over the centuries this branch of carving has been used in writing and in decoration. It just kept up with the changes of the many historical styles of art such as Renaissance, Victorian, Gothic, Art Nouveau, Art Deco, and more. By keeping up with the changes, relief carving is as relevant today as it was when the Pharaohs had their monuments decorated with hieroglyphs.

This type of carving is unique in many ways. For example, our gouges with their different shapes have been handed down to us over many generations with little change. I will show you some of these tools and teach you how to handle them. An old European master taught me the skills required. That master happened to be my father. Back when I carved with him in his studio, time seemed to stop as we carved for very long days.

When carving, you can shut the world out and forget about time. Later, when I had my own family with kids, I would escape to my studio (a tool roll and a quiet corner) and work on my carving. This brought my sanity back and gave me peace from a stressful day.

Relief carvers could be very specialized and achieved master status by reaching the highest levels of speed, excellence, and productivity. They were extremely skilled with their tools and had a vast amount of experience in the various styles of art. They could handle the many challenges that were placed before them, but talent alone could not account for their incredible skill at handling the tools so effortlessly (or so it appeared) and beautifully. Their success stemmed from being taught by other masters of relief carving and a lot of practice. The woodcarving fraternity was an extremely tight-knit group. Those who were very experienced helped the novices grow into competent carvers.

I was very fortunate to spend six years carving with my father. I now know what a privilege it was to have a skilled woodcarver by my side. I learned to handle the tools and to have complete control over the wood. When I set out on my own to support myself with my carving, I discovered the importance of the lessons learned from a master. Carving is a joy, not a struggle between tools and wood grain. When you do the exercises and projects in this book, they will teach you the ways of the old masters. You will be my apprentice. Start this carving adventure by doing the first exercises and you will end up with a beautiful crest. I think you will find the trip easier than you thought, and by the end you will find you have learned far more than you bargained for.

Don't be intimidated. This book is not going to make you a master carver overnight, but if you pay attention, I can take you to a level where you think like the old masters. I will show you how to properly handle the tools by demonstration and will show you how to approach a complex carving step by step. From my experience, this higher level of carving is rarely addressed. I will help you grow into a competent woodcarver. You will look at a complex European carving and be able to break it down into its parts and build it up into all of its glory. You will know how to begin and how to bring the work to life. You will see carvings in a whole new light and know how to see them through, no matter how complex they are.

A woodcarver is a creator. If you follow my instructions and practice, you will develop the skills needed to become a woodcarver. If I just did another beginners book, then the wood you carve will only be carved wood. However, when you get through with this book, you will be ready to take the wood and make it take on life as you see it, just as the masters before us taught their apprentices to do.

You will know when you begin to reach that creative level. Many of my students who reach that point have said, "Now I can carve anything!" The fundamentals of woodcarving will become second nature, and, through practice, the tools will begin to feel like extensions of your hands. My step-by-step logical process results in you not focusing so much on your tools or surroundings, but more on following your creative energy. That will all become second nature as your attention shifts from how you are carving to what you are carving. At this point, woodcarving/creating will take on a whole new level of enjoyment.

If you don't believe you have the talent to become a woodcarver, you are wrong. Don't ever believe that. From my experience of teaching hundreds of students before you, becoming a woodcarver has little to do with artistic ability. Many of my students discover talents that they didn't even know they had. You may have tried other art forms and they may not have gone well for you. However, with a push from this book, you just may find that woodcarving is the art form you can excel at.

From master to apprentice, you may find the knowledge and methods that will take you to the highest form of this art. I am fully convinced that these writings and exercises will inspire you to step into the wonderful world of woodcarving.

Nora's father, Johannes (Han) Leereveld in his studio circa 1950 in the Netherlands.

Chapter 1
My Life as a Woodcarver

Without question, the person most influential to my wood sculpting career is my father, Johannes Leereveld. Trained in classical relief woodcarving, he passed that knowledge on to me. Additionally, he was a very gifted teacher. The fact that he loved me dearly didn't hurt me either. I was privileged to be taught by a person who was motivated by his love for me and his desire to pass his knowledge on to the next generation.

My story is a story about someone who found her talent, listened to her teacher, and has the passion (like my father) to keep classical relief carving continuing through future generations. Therefore, my story is not over for the same reason my father's story is not over.

Born in 1922, I literally grew up around wood and art. In addition to the carving he was commissioned to make (for a living), my father carved almost all of our own furniture. It's difficult to explain, but imagine a plain dining room chair that now had leaves and scrolls rolling over its arms and legs and the top of the backrest symmetrically laced with leaves that seemed alive. Now imagine a room filled with chairs, tables, and cabinets all fully carved into masterpieces. He also had a gift for wood finishing. The grain was featured and would pop right out at you. My father didn't start out carving at home. He had to learn first, and learn he did, from carvers in the line of the old masters.

Holland had several good wood sculptors at the time. Most, like my father, worked for made-to-order companies. The customer worked with a designer until the desired pattern was agreed on. Then the designer gave the plan to a carver who would finish the project. My father was initially hired as a carver.

However, his creative talents came to the surface as he began to suggest improvements on the designs that he was given. In his mind, he knew he could have created better designs than those individuals employed by the company. It wasn't long before he realized that his dual talent would allow him to get plenty of work as an independent. His ability to design and carve allowed him to work on his own, but there was one more component to his success that caused him to be in great demand.

At the time that my father became an independent wood sculptor, the Art Nouveau Movement was still very popular, although it peaked from 1890 to 1905. Art Nouveau was an international movement that was a reaction to the academic art of the nineteenth century. It was a highly stylized floral, plant, and curvilinear type of art. For example, in regards to furniture, an Art Nouveau table would be almost completely carved with flowers, leaves, grapes, and even scroll-type lines. All over the world, Art Nouveau carvings were in high demand, highly sought after, and a sign of status, much like the paintings produced by Dutch artists, such as Rembrandt, of the seventeenth century or "The Golden Age."

Because he was very creative, my father offered designs that were true to Art Nouveau, but were clearly one-of-a-kind. As a result, he had more work than he could handle, and our family had money to spend on things beyond the everyday necessities. For example, we bought a cabin cruiser. Our favorite vacation was on the waterways of Holland.

With all of this art around me, I don't ever remember at the time thinking about carving or handling wood myself, although teaching art crossed my mind. The general track most girls took in those days was to get married and raise a family. Even though there were many women who attended institutions of higher education, most ended up with administrative-type work until they found a man and got married. I was very different. I thought differently. My dreams were different. At the time, my father inspired me to become something more than a wife and mother. I wanted a family, but at the same time I wanted a taste of what my father demonstrated, which was to get paid for doing something you love. I was alive and the world was mine, that is, until the Great Depression.

Suddenly, the world was changing quickly. Although Holland had its trade with its East India and West India colonies to maintain a higher standard of living than most of Europe, we did not escape the Great Depression altogether. Unemployment was at an all-time high. The demand for my father's carving was drying up quickly, and, at one point, almost stopped altogether.

Germany was taking over country after country. When they finally invaded Holland, things became very different and difficult for us. Initially, we lived close to Amsterdam so that my brother and I could continue our education, but, because food was scarce in the city, we moved to the country where we could grow our own food. We moved to the small village of Blaricum where, by chance, there was a healthy concentration of artists. We felt right at home there. It was one of the most beautiful spots in Holland and still is today.

There, we could live off the land. Those that owned stores, however, found themselves quickly without product as the Germans either stole or bought them out. Because the Germans had put a stop to all importing, there was no way to replenish what they had taken. As a result, all of us lived on the food we could grow. The Germans bought what we grew and exported it to Germany. So, there was no way to save or store food for the future, especially for the winter. There was no fat or meat, but, once in a while, we could get fish for protein. We were always hungry, skinny, but healthy. I thank God for that.

We made salads with greens from our garden, and my father made delicious sauerkraut with our homegrown cabbage. Even in the area of food, my father's creativity surfaced. He made incredibly tasty sauerkraut from endive and other vegetables.

Although the Dutch woodcarvers were immersed in Classical Art Nouveau, the Germans preferred the Gothic style, and it became popular. Gothic carvings are very heavy, preferably made from oak, and required extensive carving and detail. This was right up my father's alley. He had more work than he could handle.

One day in 1941, at 11:00 am, right in the middle of carving, my father asked me, "Nora, why don't you try your hands on a tool and do some carving?" I did. I loved it so much I stayed at the workbench until 10:00 pm, only interrupted by lunch and dinner. I loved it and couldn't stop.

Beginning with simple designs, I learned the basics quickly. It wasn't long before I found myself helping my father carve panels, drawer fronts, sides of chairs, chandeliers, all in Gothic style. We carved church-style arches, rosettes, spandrels, linenfolds, and lots of crests. We designed and carved them all. Crests were some of my favorites because there is no limit to their variety. Some are: Stars, Beams, Roosters, and all sorts of Animals and Shields. I was in heaven because the customers allowed me to use my imagination and creativity to arrive at designs. In the framework of the Gothic style, we came up with hundreds of ideas, many by searching through books.

As I look back on the beginning of my carving career, I remember the teaching genius of my father. Here I was working from dawn to dusk, improving with every stroke of the tool, and he rarely paid me a compliment. He corrected me often, and, when I learned a particular skill, he simply gave me something even more difficult to do. Like all great teachers, he knew what motivated his student to continually improve. Apparently, I was motivated by progress and corrective guidance rather than compliments.

His criticism was sometimes very harsh, but it shaped me artistically. For example, I remember carving a leaf that I was very proud of. In boast, I showed it to him and to my surprise he called it a "beefsteak." He explained that I had learned all the basics of carving, but my leaf had no life. What he continued to show me was the difference between "copying" and "creating." He went on to explain, copying is necessary when you are a novice, but one must advance to a new level if one is to become an "artist." It was my first lesson in the real art of wood sculpturing.

I learned that the lines that you use to lay out a carving may limit your imagination if you're not careful. A focus on the pattern rather than the real object can quench any chance for creating the illusion of movement, an essential for giving life to an object.

Beginning with a general idea of the shape of a leaf, for example, and carving out an outline with, what we carvers call, a "V-tool," I began to create life. This is what I teach today. Begin with copying, but advance to art. Students that "get it" learn to see in their mind's eyes a real leaf and learn to create what they see. They realize a leaf is not flat. Its edges dip and rise like the ocean's swells. The main vein is not a straight line. It curves as it is influenced by the movement of the edges and vice versa. Once I learned that, my carving went to another level. My tools began to shape and mold the wood until flowers were blooming and leaves were gently flowing.

When my father and I were caught up with our work (which rarely happened), we started thinking out of the box and creating things. I remember working in clay to produce molds for elaborate frames from classical French periods. One hilarious thing, now that I look back on it, was making carvings we passed on as antiques and fooled Germans into thinking they were. We sculptured religious statues, about one and one-half feet in height. We spotted them with gold, red, and/or green oil paint, and they began to look like they were old and worn. Then, to finish the job, we buried them in the wet, Dutch, soil for a few weeks, and, when we took them out and wiped them down, they looked like antiques. How I chuckled when a German would pay a price well above value for one of those statues that, just a few weeks before, was simply a piece of wood.

When the war ended and we were all convinced it would take a long time to rebuild Holland, thousands emigrated to foreign shores. Finding a new life across the sea is not new to the Dutch; we have been doing that for centuries, and it is a reason the Dutch are considered innovators, explorers, and people of ingenuity. They had to be. Perhaps it's our small country or perhaps it's a desire for an improved standard of living, but the Dutch are a people that are not afraid to face danger and death to get ahead. That was the mindset of the Dutch during the Golden Age, and also that of the Dutch after World War II. It was time to find somewhere with new opportunities and somewhere to prosper. I chose the United States of America.

In December of 1956 my husband, youngest son, and I crossed the Atlantic on Holland America's *Zuiderkruis*, a relatively small ship. Bobbling over huge waves and, at times, fearing for our lives, it took two weeks before we landed in New York harbor on New Year's Eve. We traveled by train to Phoenix, Arizona, with $14 in our pockets.

As is true today, in order to immigrate into the United States, one must have a sponsor, a person or family, that takes responsibility to ensure success. One thing the US government wants to avoid is an immigrant's failure and having to go back. Our sponsor was a Phoenix-based Quaker group. We made friends quickly, and I got my first carving job within months—a Book of Remembrance for the First Presbyterian Church in downtown Phoenix. This book served as a guest log that visitors signed when entering the church. The most notable signature in the book belongs to President Lyndon Johnson. The book is still on display in the entrance hall, featuring his signature.

Eventually, we moved to Southern California. We found, when you have uprooted yourself from your birthplace, it becomes easier to relocate. There are so many interesting places in America, each with unique history, opportunities, and adventure. Everywhere I've traveled, I have found beautiful people, new neighbors, and friends.

As you might imagine, when I left Holland, I made sure to pack all my tools, mallets, and the carving patterns that I had accumulated over the years. I had no workbench, however. Fortunately, the Phoenix Elks Club put one together for me. It did the job for the time being, but I wanted a custom-made bench. My wish took years to materialize, but it finally happened in Southern California. With a height of 42 inches, it was perfect.

With the perfect bench, I was ready to expand my business. It wasn't long until I was taking orders from all over the country. Wineries, individuals, and companies placed orders, and I became very busy. Even Hugh Hefner commissioned me to do extensive carvings in the Playboy Mansion, in Bel Air.

As my work increased in popularity, people became interested, not only in purchasing my work, but learning how to carve. That's when I realized I should begin teaching. I found myself teaching within the Adult Education System. My classes became so popular that they were often overbooked.

At the time, many Americans tried to learn relief carving on their own, only to become frustrated and give up. Some of them learned about my classes, and their passion was reborn when I showed them how to do it. My classes became an "eye opener" for them. When they learned the basics of carving, as I did from my father, they realized it was easier to do than they thought it would be.

In short, I began to feel the joy of teaching. I wanted to continue and improve. I wanted more people to learn. So, with the help of my family, I created several "how to" videos/DVD's and a website, www.norahall.com. Suddenly, my teaching was in demand all over the country.

My son Wendell is a gifted artist in his own right. He's a natural. I hardly had to teach him to carve. At one point, he began working in clay. Many of his creations ended up being carved in wood. He helped me with many carving projects, much like I helped my father. It was then that I fully realized the joy my father felt when he worked with me.

Nora Hall Carving Designs became, and still is, a family business. My daughter, Renée, is largely responsible for getting it off the ground. My grandchildren even helped, especially with the website. Wendell was responsible for producing the nine videos. I believe my father would have been proud.

I have never forgotten where I came from, and, for that reason, have appreciated what I have. While carving, my father and I wore wooden shoes filled with straw to keep our feet warm. We had no heat in the workshop. Things got worse every year of the war. The infamous "Hunger Winter," (when there was absolutely nothing left) resulted in thousands of urban people dying of starvation. Our lives were threatened every day. Young men were transported to Germany to work in factories. As a result, men grew beards to appear older. People were hiding. The worst of it was how the Germans pursued the Jewish people. They had become scapegoats to rationalize the

Nazi belief in a dominant race and the survival of the fittest and strongest. We hid Jewish families under our living room floor while Germans searched above them. My brother was working for the resistance. Had he been caught, all of us would have been dragged away to concentration camps.

But it was our work that kept us sane, gave us hope, and saved us in many ways. Another silver lining was the close relationship my father and I had. He just loved working with me, and, believe me, the feeling was mutual. I was very lucky.

Before his death in 1995, my father came to America two times to visit. He even visited my wood sculpturing classes. Can you imagine what joy that brought to me? Well into his eighties, and not able to speak English, he won the respect of my students by demonstrating techniques and passing on his words of wisdom that I interpreted. The students were amazed and demonstrated their appreciation by arranging potluck dinners, an American tradition he had never experienced. And I? I was reminded of how gifted he was, both as a carver and a teacher. He reminded me of the attention to details—one difference between a good carver and a great one.

While in America, he began sharpening my tools, something he used to do in the old days. He sharpened tools in the old way, working on a perfect bevel and then honing for hours, just like the masters did before him. Back in Holland, he had different shapes and grits of handstones, flat and also with rounded edges for the inside bevels of the various sweeps of tools. For example, there was a sharp edged stone for the V-tool, a tool in the shape of the letter V. It's used to cut sharp lines into wood. He worked for hours on the tools, honing the burrs back and forth until the edge was completely smooth. Some carvers cut corners by breaking a burr off, not my father. When I was his apprentice he used to keep all my tools sharp. That was a regular practice as we worked a lot in hard woods, such as Oak and Birch, that would damage the edges of the tools.

As I watched my father sharpen my tools once again, I was reminded of one thing—the mastering of the grain. If you cut against the grain, chipping is very likely to occur, ruining the design you have in mind. In my early years, I would make mistakes like that and thought I would never master this obstacle.

What helped me was becoming ambidextrous, a skill pivotal to proper and quick carving. It makes it a little easier to master the grain when one can change directions and maintain momentum.

As I watched him, I was also reminded that when I emigrated to the US without my father (who had always sharpened my tools), I needed to find a more efficient way to sharpen my tools. I have met many American carvers, most of them not involved in classical relief carving, but I learned something very valuable from them. They used a belt sander to start the tool sharpening process. By using a belt sander with 100 grit paper, one can make a perfect bevel on a tool. After forming the correct bevel, a burr is formed along the edge of the blade. Removing that burr with a honing stone seemed to take forever. I now use two types of buffing wheels with abrasives to achieve a final edge to the blade. In a matter of seconds you will create the sharpest edge without turning the tool over. I sell these wheels and abrasive compounds on my website.

My point is, I value the meticulous ways to sharpen tools. I saw my father sharpen tools when I was younger and now use a faster process. By using the newer sharpening methods, I don't believe I have sacrificed anything nor have I compromised the spirit, importance, and quality of proper tool sharpening.

From my father, I learned there is a proper way to do everything, from sharpening tools to carving. That "proper way" has been around for centuries. My father learned from the masters, and I learned from him. And now it's my turn. Like Johannes Leereveld, I have a burning need to pass on what I learned from my father and what he learned from the masters.

Chapter 2
The German Occupation

I had my whole life planned out, but the situations you experience during life can sure change the best laid plans. I lived on the outskirts of Amsterdam with my mother, father, and brother. I had just finished our five years of high school, and the day I rode my bicycle into Amsterdam to take my exams was the day the German military began to bomb our country, starting with the biggest city, Amsterdam. The German soldiers wanted our country, which was so close to theirs. I can't describe the sheer terror of trying to get home from my tests, on a bicycle, with bombs dropping all around me.

I was going to be an art teacher, and, after high school and a few more years of higher education, I was sure to teach. Suddenly we became a highly valued target to the German war machine. They had no cold water port. They could flood most of the lowlands, if need be, by using the levies we built to protect the low lands and, in that way, stop the British from invading Europe from our direction. Their decision to invade Holland ended my formal education and started my apprenticeship in woodcarving.

Our country was relatively defenseless, so the German war machine quickly took the Netherlands (more commonly known as Holland). The intensity and severity of danger was so great that the word, "fear" just doesn't seem to capture the feelings of the people during the period of German occupation. The Germans were cold blooded killers and they were always walking around everywhere looking for young men for their war factories and anyone else breaking a whole list of new rules such as no electricity, no radios, no people of Jewish descent, and so much more. We were terrified of them, and that is just the way they wanted us to be.

I realize that the people of the USA were aware of the brutality of war. They had Pearl Harbor to show them how ruthless the enemy could be in times of war. They had to send their young men off to war in Europe and the South Pacific without knowing whether those young men would ever come back, and, if they came back, would they ever be the same? We in Holland saw the war on a daily basis and lived in terror day after day. People were shot for no reason at all except to prove that the Germans were in charge.

In 1940, shortly after the war broke out in Holland, my father, mother, brother, and I escaped the danger of living in Amsterdam and moved to an affluent area called Blaricum. Even to this day, Blaricum is one of the richest and most beautiful areas of Holland. The country is bent on keeping it this way since building permits are almost impossible to come by.

We lived in a house that was divided. There was the front of the house that was very large and looked like the entire house. Then there was the back of the house which was smaller and often overlooked by the Germans. An old actor lived in the front part of the house and used its large size to hide Jewish families who were always on their way to somewhere else. We lived in the back part of the house, and, although smaller, we still had good hiding places for those not wishing to be seen by the Germans.

Like I said before, we lived in the terror of war every day. I would have a hard time putting the dangerous and intense atmosphere we experienced during those years on paper. Whatever you read, whatever movie you have seen, understand it was much more intense and all of our senses were at peak performance, even to the point of exhaustion, at all times. If not, if one mistake was made, somebody was either taken away and/or killed. The German soldiers had no tolerance, no empathy, and no patience at all.

Randomly and periodically, German soldiers performed "searches." No part of Holland was exempt from this procedure. As a result, the privacy we all take for granted was gone. Any house, store, or barn could be searched for no reason, and at any time. You knew every soldier you saw in the street or on the bus was well-trained. When you saw them standing outside your door, telling you they were going to come in, you knew those soldiers wouldn't think twice about taking you away. If you were involved in "illegal activities," like hiding people or radios, or made any wrong move or noise, you were gone. You were looking into the eyes of trained killers, and you were not on their side of their law. Your heart felt like it was in your throat, and you could hear it beat faster and faster.

The Germans tried hard to make the random searches a surprise, but the underground, our resistance fighters, had infiltrated the German Intelligence at about every level. Therefore, we would get warnings as to what the Germans were up to on a given day. My brother, Marcel, was a fit young man, so, if caught on the street, he would be put to work in a German war factory (war factories that the US Air Force was busy bombing off the face of the earth). Since he didn't like anything the German Army was doing to anyone, he joined the resistance. Many a time we hid him in the attic between the roof tiles and the attic itself, where he couldn't be seen or, unfortunately, be very comfortable.

Since we lived in the small part of the back of the main house, the Germans often overlooked our small living quarters, thinking it was just part of the large main house. But we knew that when a warning came down that the Germans were on the way, we could lose all of our possessions, and if they found the radios we had hidden or a person we were protecting, our lives could change drastically. They could send us to a concentration camp, and no one came back from them. They could put us to work in their factories that needed young Gentiles, or a soldier could just shoot anyone on the spot to make an example out of them for all to see.

When we knew a certain part of our village was about to be searched, the Jews and young men fled to other homes or moved to more secure places in the houses. These more secure places were great places to hide, so we tried to use them for only 24 hours or less. My brother would be in his place between the roof and roof tiles of our neighbors, not able to move. The actor in the front house and our family in the back house soon had a reputation for helping those who needed hiding. The house was often filled to capacity, front and back.

During these days, we were filled with fear, not only for the people we hid but for ourselves as well. No Dutch person refused to help save lives, even at the risk of their own. We were compelled to do the right thing, and, in doing the right thing, there are moments that we forgot the risks to our own lives as we tried to save others. There was nothing in it for us other than the peace in knowing you are human and part of a greater good than yourself. You are on the right side of humanity, morality, and ethics. The Germans couldn't take that away from us.

Germany was in a depression when they started this war. So, when they got to Amsterdam, they were amazed at how full our stores were. We had fresh meats and cheeses and so much more. The Germans began to buy everything in sight with German Marks. As they threw people out of their houses, the Germans became thieves. Luckily for us, the store owners hid all they could for their Dutch customers. The Germans did not take long to empty out all the stores and send everything to Germany.

Supporting more than ourselves, and under the oppressive eyes of the Germans, meant we would be out of food before long. We began planting gardens in our yards with the hope of getting through this war without starving. Even with these preparations, we began to run out of food. As stated before, the last winter of the war became known as "The Hunger Winter". Food became very hard to come by. The German Army did not get any more supplies from Germany. Thousands of people were leaving the cities in search of food. What food we had we shared with the poor refugees. Eventually, we had to head out to the country, on foot or on bicycle, to see if the farmers could help us.

The Germans and the winter left Holland with almost nothing. There was not even enough wood to build coffins and bodies were wrapped in whatever blankets people could spare and buried in the ground. Most of Holland is below sea level and the parts that are not below sea level are still wet most of the time. I don't need to go into graphic details about the wet soil and the bodies buried in blankets. Where we lived, the land was part of the original Holland, so the area was slightly above sea level. The Dutch increased their land to areas below sea level. This was done by building dykes and pumping the water back out into the North Sea. We stayed relatively dry, but we began to hear stories of what was happening with the bodies in the wet cemeteries. To make matters worse, during that last period of the war, the Germans flooded parts of Western Holland by just letting the water of the North Sea stream into our low lands. They wanted to prevent the Allied Forces from attacking and freeing us by making it impossible for them to land on our shores by sea or air.

"The Hunger Winter" was made worse by the Germans in other ways, too. The Allied Forces were going straight to Berlin and defeating Germans on their own turf, but Holland was still very much occupied by the Germans (Germans retreated into western Holland), and Holland was isolated and somewhat forgotten. With food scarce and more people coming in, starvation became a real threat. The Germans hoarded almost all of the food for themselves.

People find ways to survive. On my bicycle, I rode 100 kilometers (62 miles) each way, into the country to find farmers who still had food. I made the trips about once a week. I had a little platform in front of my handle bars to carry food on. Sometimes I rode home with a chicken hanging over my handle bars. As time went on, I became an expert at loading food on my bike like grain and potatoes. I was also an expert at hiding meat on myself, such as wrapping bacon around my waist and placing a piece of ham on my stomach. The Germans would have taken the meat so I came back fat and frumpy looking. I would have never won a beauty contest, but, for the times, I was definitely the best dressed. Everyone in our area was anticipating my return. I would give everything to my parents first, and, when they had what they needed, I shared the rest.

My bicycle trips were not without personal danger. Between the farms and the village I lived in was a German check point. Everyone had to stop and be searched. Whatever the Germans wanted they just took. I knew they didn't want potatoes but would take bacon or other meats. I would hide bacon inside of the potatoes or even in the pedals on my bike. Anything I could think of doing to get my food through the check point, I did. Once I got down the road and out of sight, I could retrieve my food from the odd hiding places on my bike. Most of the time the soldiers would let me through without question, even when they saw I had some food on my bicycle. I had no way around showing some food like grain or potatoes, but with the meats I took no chances.

There was a lot of tension and danger on my trips to the farms. The trip was long, and sometimes I felt like a Brinks truck with all I was carrying, both hidden and in view. On such long trips I would get hungry. One time I was so hungry that I decided to eat something on the road. I got out a piece of bread and some smoked bacon. As I began eating the sandwich I had made, a young man approached me. He asked if he could have a bite. Feeling guilty, I gave him half of my sandwich. As soon as he began to eat his half, more people started showing up.

Hungry people started to gather all around me. They were still on their way to the farmers and starving. I didn't want to refuse a hungry person a bite to eat, but I could not afford to give away all the food that I had worked so hard to get. My parents were counting on me. My friends and neighbors were counting on me. The longer I stood still, the more people began to show up. I had to get on my bike and move on while they all changed their attention from me to the young man eating the sandwich.

On another trip to the country, I became so hungry that I walked up to a farmhouse and asked if they had any extra food. Luck was on my side when I found out that the farmhands had just finished eating and I was allowed to spoon out the remains in the pan. The pan had oatmeal in it. That was the best oatmeal I had ever had. The oats were fresh from the farm.

I remember some very scary and very sad sights as I traveled into the country. German airplanes would swoop down from sky and shoot at us, killing people left and right. This made me sense what little price the Germans placed on our lives. I was always aware of the best places to hide just in case a plane came along. There were ditches on the side of the roads near the cities. But most were filled with rainwater. All along the way lived compassionate farmers that looked out for us.

More and more the people I met on the road who had left their homes to find food were from Den Haag or Rotterdam, a large city in southern Holland. I met a woman that had walked all the way from Rotterdam, leaving her husband and baby, just to find food. She was pushing a baby buggy that had lost three wheels and was trying to find a way to fill the buggy with food so she could take it home and feed her family. Her husband couldn't make the trip because, if he had been spotted by the Germans, he would have been forced to work in a German war factory. Sadly, many of our young men died when the Allied Forces bombed the German war factories.

What you read in a history book of World War II is just a small part of the story. Living the war was so different, so horrific. I could go on and on with memories like these. Thinking back to that time brings back so many terrible memories.

The underground was extremely active during the war. There was no communication in our country to know what was going on in the real world, only what the Germans wanted us to know, or so they believed. The purpose of my trips throughout the countryside was not limited to searching for food. I was also distributing illegal literature with the latest news and encouragement from the outside world. I wasn't the only one. We all carried the latest news, whether written or verbal. Some of us learned things directly from the underground (remember, my brother was a member), and we spread the news, which traveled like a chain reaction. News was constantly flowing from the source out to the people across the country. The travelers like me spread the news from village to village, and the villagers told each other. This made for a lot of camaraderie, conversation, and friendships along the way. In a real sense, those of us who traveled were the newspapers and radios of Holland in the days when the Germans thought they controlled all information.

The underground did a lot throughout the war. Early on, before "The Hunger Winter," my boyfriend and I made trips throughout the countryside of Holland to spread the news of the day. After asking the farmers for permission, we would sleep in haystacks as we traveled. Somewhere in the middle of the country (I don't remember exactly where), we approached a farm to ask if we could spend the night. A man stopped us from coming any closer and asked why we were there. We thought it an odd question but he would not let us take one more step before he was sure we were not the enemy. After finishing his detailed interview and confident we were who we said we were, he told us why he had to interrogate us. He told us that on the very spot he was standing, the very spot that we would have to walk over to get in the farm house, he could disappear into the ground. He didn't say more but we were pretty sure there was a hollowed out area under the ground cover where goods delivered by English planes would disappear almost instantly. The underground was that organized and effective, even that early in the war.

The flow of up-to-date information and the knowledge that the underground was so powerful gave us hope that someday Holland would be free again. If you have ever been in a seemingly hopeless situation, where you don't really know how things will turn out, and all you can think is the worst, you will begin to understand how all the Dutch people felt during the war. We could have easily lost all hope because Germany was so powerful, and the German propaganda was forced on everyone. Thank God for the underground and all of us who never stopped believing. That was the thing that kept us alive and kept us looking forward to a better day to come.

We were very grateful for the Allied Forces. The Germans had large lights and big guns to knock airplanes out of the sky. I remember seeing planes flying over our heads at night, lit up by the German lights, and hearing the big guns going off. But those American planes flew too high for the German guns. The big planes flew over Holland on their way to some place in Germany. Late in the war, the Germans based their fighter planes at our airport. When the American planes flew over, the German fighters went up to shoot them down. I remember seeing the sparks from the German fighters, and the American planes exploding. The planes would break into pieces and everything was on fire. If airmen could jump from the planes, the big German guns shot at the parachutes until they folded up, and the airmen would either be dead or plunge to their deaths. I knew I wasn't the only one watching. People all over Holland saw the same thing.

We had to hold onto every positive experience to get through the darkest times of the war. Those Allied planes, the food I was able to get home during that last winter, and the radio my Dad hid under the floorboards all helped us cope with the terror that we experienced during the German occupation. We knew that we were not alone, and Allied planes and information dispelled the German propaganda. What a comfort it was to know that the world was not going to put up with tyranny. Many died trying to stop the Germans from reaching their objectives, and those of us who wouldn't let the Germans win in Holland are so thankful for all of them. We are thankful for all the people that rose up and fought the Germans. We hung onto any positive experience we had, and that made us stronger. If you survived Holland during those terrible years, you could survive anything, believe me.

Dutch people have something in them that gives them the urge to travel and see the world. I don't know if it is the size of the country or it being just in their nature. After the war, my Dutch instincts told me to leave the Old World and move to the New World, America. That was not easy, but with freedom, after having been through the war, a person believes they can accomplish anything, especially after being told what and what not to do on a daily basis.

I made it to America several years later. As a result of my experiences during the war, I am a very independent woman. I am self-employed, and, not too surprisingly, I am self-sufficient and independent. I have raised my children to be self-sufficient and independent. That is probably not surprising when you are molded by poverty, uncertainty, fear, and a desire to survive. Do I have any regrets? Yes, I regret that I couldn't have saved more lives and rescued more people during the war. But I'll bet that anyone who was there has the same regret.

Chapter 3
The Methods of the Masters
How to Grip the Tool

When you carve wood, you need to have absolute control over your tools. You can not afford to put hours into a carving only to cut off a critical part near the end and have to start all over again. When you quote a price for a carving, you need to take into account the skill level or how difficult the work will be, how many hours the woodcarving will take you, and the cost of the supplies (wood, etc.). If you carve for three weeks and then make a bad slip with the tool, as we all have, then you have to decide if you are able to fix it. If that is impossible, you have to start all over and lose everything that you have invested.

To become a master, you must first master your tools. You need to know how to use them to your best ability regardless of how hard the wood is to work with, regardless of the wood grain (which your tool will follow rather than cutting through), regardless of the wood. This is no light topic. However, I learned the ways that have been passed down from the master carvers of Europe. We will devote this chapter to the methods of how to use professional size woodcarving tools, mainly the tool grips that will give you full control of the cutting edge.

Fig. 3.1: Here is a very comfortable way for a right-handed person to hold the tool. If you are left-handed, just reverse the hands. The right hand holds the handle of the tool. The end of the handle fits in the palm of the right hand. The fingers of the left hand wrap around part of the handle and most of the metal blade of the tool almost to the cutting edge with the thumb going up the handle. The left wrist rests on the wood for tool control.

Fig. 3.2: This is the back view of Fig. 3.1. The left hand is on the left and you can see the fingers wrapped around the metal blade of the tool and also some of the handle. The thumb of that hand goes straight up the handle. On the right you can see the right hand cupping the handle end of the tool so that it can push the tool through the wood.

Fig. 3.3: This shows the tool cutting into the wood. The left hand is wrapped around the metal blade with the thumb going up the handle. My right hand thumb is on top of my left thumb. My right hand index finger must rest on top of the tool handle, even under my left hand, if necessary.

The tool is firmly held by my left hand and the left wrist should rest on the wood that you are working on at all times. If possible you should rest your wrist and entire forearm down on the work. While you carve, you put pressure on the tool with your left hand. You push down with your right hand but maintain pressure with your left hand to keep the tool in control. The left hand is wrapped around the tool. Your left wrist is resting on the carving. Your left hand is your control hand. Your right hand is in a position to push the tool. Move the tool with the right hand and control the tool with your left.

Replace the right hand with a mallet and all the conditions are the same. The right hand moves the tool (with a mallet), and your left hand is anchored to the carving to give you the ultimate control. Movement and control; reverse the hands and the right hand is wrapped around the tool and anchored to the carving for control and the left hand is on the tool handle top to push or use a mallet. Again, you have movement and control.

However, when you have to change hands and the mallet is now in your left hand, it can feel very awkward when you are right-handed. The only cure is practice. After about one hour of carving left-handed, you should get used to it. If you are left-handed and switch to right-handed carving, which is necessary to be a good carver, an efficient carver, then put the mallet in your right hand and practice, practice, practice. Soon you will be able to switch from right to left without thinking about it. I always say that this will take about one hour because when I teach students they usually can carve both handed within about that time.

If you feel a twitch of pain or fatigue in your lower back, then you know why your work bench has to be at the proper height. You should be in a comfortable position, forearm down and all.

 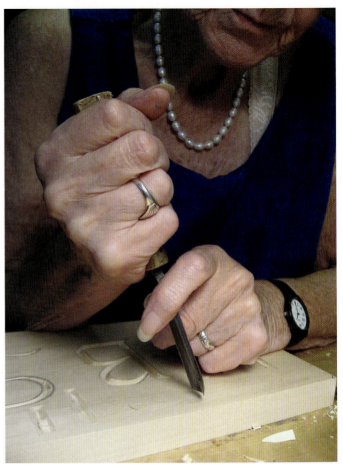

Fig. 3.4: There is one more tool hold you need to know. I use this tool grip in both letter carving and in doing outline cuts. The outline cuts are used to finish up or clean up a carving by generally cutting straight down. Again I will describe this from the right-handed point of view. If you are left-handed, just reverse the hands.

I grip the blade of the tool with the left hand thumb and index finger to hold the blade in place. I hold the tool handle with my right hand to direct the tool in carving. With my right hand on the handle I can turn the tool, push the cutting edge into the wood, and do all the motions required to make the cuts I need, mostly push cuts. Note that I keep my left hand anchored on the workpiece.

Fig. 3.5: Again, I am holding the blade of the tool between the thumb and index finger of my left hand (my second finger also helps align the blade), and hold the handle with my right hand, rest my left hand on the wood, and I manipulate the tool with my right hand. Here I am using part of the cutting edge to slice forward.

Practice these tool grips and you will find you will have control over your cutting edge. With this kind of control, you will be able to carve in comfort and without worry of destroying a beautiful work of art after so many hours of precise carving. Do not fear left and right hand carving because, as I said, my students seem to get this down with good effect after only one hour of practice. So study, practice, and enjoy!

Chapter 4
Seventeenth Century Dutch Panel

Through my many travels teaching woodcarving all across this great country, I've met a lot of people. As you can well imagine, every student has a story. Their stories are all quite interesting and usually tell me of the events in their lives that resulted in them wanting to learn woodcarving and how they ended up in my class. I find their stories unique and wonderful.

Stories are not limited to just people. Things have stories too. Houses, bicycles, dolls, and even a hat can have a story. How many times have you heard, "If these walls could talk"? If only my tools could talk! Carvings have stories too. This seventeenth century hand-carved panel has had quite a long history, if it could only talk. I'd like to share with you a part of the panel's tale as it relates to me.

My woodcarving friends invited me to their studio in Amsterdam a few years before I would emigrate from Holland. As I walked in, I noticed a beautiful piece they had hanging on the wall. Looking at it closer I saw that it was made of plaster. So I asked them to tell me more about this interesting design.

My friends told me that the panel was from the door of a seventeenth century home near the center of Amsterdam on one of the many canals. They wanted to preserve, and carve for themselves, this wonderful example of seventeenth century Dutch woodcarving. They went up to the door in the middle of the night, when there was no one to question their intentions, and they made a mold of it!

First, they applied talcum powder on the door panel. Then, they pushed sculptor's clay hard into the panel. The talcum powder made the clay peel off easily. The result was a perfect mold. From the mold they made plaster copies which they used as models to carve the panel from.

They gave me a plaster copy. I took it with me in my personal belongings (not in my luggage) to this country on the Dutch ship *Zuiderkruis* for the trip to New York and then from there to Phoenix, Arizona, by train. I made it to my destination, and the 9" x 12" plaster model did not have a single chip in it! I have since carved the beautiful design in many different woods and have taught quite a number of my students how to do the same.

The composition of this ornamental design is quite interesting. Two vines cross each other at one end and climb around the sides in opposite directions giving the foliage and a cluster of grapes plenty of room to unfold. They are balanced out by the center ribbon that draws our eyes to the center and holds the entire pattern together. The flowing shape of the ribbon creates ample opportunity for the carver to show off his or her skills in linenfold carving. The leaves on this panel have a very basic shape, almost stylized. This strongly represents the Gothic influence that was still present, if only for a little longer, in Northern Europe in the seventeenth century.

To give this panel a good start, we should make the background quite deep. You want to give the branches, foliage, and ribbon enough material to overlay at different depths and make it possible for some leaves to dip into the background and come up gracefully in a natural movement and flow.

The most important part of carving this project will be to bring movement and shape to the vines, leaves, and ribbon. We call this the sculpturing of this carving. This means leaves that look lifelike, branches that move in and around as in nature, and a ribbon that flows naturally. This makes all the difference in the end product.

Start this carving by outlining with a V-tool, not stab cuts (or stop cuts), to leave enough wood to make slight changes at different depths possible, if needed. After outlining with the V-tool, we go over the whole carving with bold cuts, both high and low, sculpting the individual parts and how they interact. The original drawing should be in front of you at all times. Be ready with a pencil to fill the details back in after we cut off the lines as we sculpt.

Like most grape leaves, each leaf consists of three leaflets and two round lobes, one on each side of the stem. These leaves are interpretations of nature from a certain time in history in Europe. They are unique and attractive. Clever balance was incorporated in this panel by having most of the leaves moving towards the right while the ribbon is unfurling to the left. Balance was even incorporated in the way the branches are broken off here and there at just the right locations. We would have a hard time changing the arrangement of this composition and improving on it.

The applications of this panel are endless. Not only can this design decorate exterior doors but also cabinet doors, and, on a smaller scale, jewelry boxes. The design is complete enough to stand on its own. It would make a beautiful wall hanging. If you do use it as a wall hanging, please don't add a frame. This beautiful design needs no assistance. I know because when I walked into my friends' woodcarving studio so long ago in Amsterdam, this beautiful design stood out and sure caught my attention!

Carving a Seventeenth Century Dutch Panel:
Carving Exercises 1 and 2

The following exercises are designed to show you how to carve, step by step, two details of a ribbon before you start the panel. The seventeenth century Dutch Panel has such a pronounced, beautiful ribbon crossing it, that is what catches the viewer's attention. Your eye is drawn towards it. So, by practicing these two critical areas of the ribbon first, you will be well prepared for carving the complete carving.

If you want to see me actually carving a ribbon, also called a linenfold, you may purchase my DVD called *Carving the Linenfold with Nora Hall* at www.norahall.com.

Exercise 1

Fig. 4.1: The pattern is drawn on the wood, ready to carve. Go to page 24 for the complete pattern. The pattern dimensions are 9.4" x 12". Make sure to orient the pattern to the wood grain as shown here. Orient the wood itself to you as shown in Fig. 4.1. Then, if I say carve up, you know I mean to carve from the bottom of the picture to the top.

Fig. 4.2: Using a 39-10mm V-tool (75 degree V-tool), I have gone over all the lines of the drawing. Place the tool right on the line so as not to enlarge the pattern.

Fig. 4.3: I rough the wood away from the ribbon with a deep gouge, (9-12mm).

Fig. 4.4: I deepen the V cut around the ribbon with a narrower V-tool (60 degrees). I use a 41-10mm V-tool. I cut deeper but do not cut into to ribbon. If you do not have a 41 V-tool, use your 39 V-tool, but keep one side tilted away from the ribbon to avoid cutting it. I don't want to cut into the ribbon at this point, so I don't make the cut across it any deeper. Also, you want to deepen the outline, not make the ribbon narrower with this pass.

Continue deepening around the ribbon with a 9-12mm. I lower the top of the left side of the ribbon with a 5-12mm to begin the look of the left side going under the right. Notice how I continue this across the bottom to carve the entire left side of the ribbon. I stop to push upward with the 5 sweep, being careful to leave the very right edge of the bottom part to rise up. Then, smooth the left ribbon side with the 3-12mm.

Fig. 4.5: One cut upward with a 9-12mm (or a 10-12mm) to make the top layer of the curl.

Fig.4.6: Using an 11-3mm to make short hollow cuts, one on each corner where the ribbon curls over itself. To make these very delicate, short hollow cuts, slice upwards and then with the grain. Study the picture well. These are a very important couple of cuts! They give the illusion of the folding motion of the scroll.

Fig. 4.7: Finish the ribbon with a flat tool (2 1/2 or 3 sweep) to smooth out the edges and tuck the left hand side of the ribbon under the right hand side of the ribbon.

A NOTE ON TOOLS: I will try to use the tools in my recommended tool set. Where appropriate, I will use a tool outside my recommended set. If you do not have that tool, then use the tools you have to your best advantage. If I am using a deep tool from my set, use the deep tool you have. If I am using a shallow tool, use the shallow tool you have. You do not have to have every tool made, but you do have to have enough tools. Without enough tools, carving can become more difficult. For example, if I am using a 3-20mm and the closest tool you have is a 3-10mm you will have to do a lot of extra work to achieve what I can in a few calculated moves. How do you know what "enough tools" are? Only carving will tell you if you really need that tool or this tool.

Exercise 2:

Repeat and practice, I cannot say enough that good woodcarving comes from practice, practice, practice! Carve these two exercises as many times as necessary for you to feel comfortable carving them and you consistently get clean, crisp carvings. When carving the final project, you will have only one chance to get these ribbon parts right. Also, take careful note of my tool holding techniques. The way I hold a carving tool means no wrong cuts, no slips of the tool, only completely controlled carving. Pay close attention and apply these techniques for the best results.

Fig. 4.9: The lines are cut with a 39-10mm V-tool as in exercise 1. The V-tool continues the lines of the innermost roll all the way off the scroll since that will all stay at the same depth. The wood surrounding the ribbon is lowered with a 9-12mm or a similar deep tool. You will find the complete pattern on page 24.

Fig. 4.8: A pattern for this exercise is located in Appendix B. Use the lower portion of the linenfold for this exercise. The pattern shown on the wood is in the orientation that it should be to you the carver. So carving up means from the bottom of the picture up to the top of the picture. This is a very important part of the ribbon, so it will make excellent practice.

Fig.4.10: Using a 5-6mm, remove wood from the inside of the inner roll to open it up and give it shape. Use the 11-6mm to push upward at a slight angle that is the center of the innermost roll to give it that three-dimensional shape with the bottom low and the sides up. Notice how nicely the end of the ribbon (the right side of the inner most roll) stands up.

Fig. 4.11: Use the 11-3mm to make the short delicate cut up, and then with the grain along the inside lip of the inner roll first from the left and then the right to create the illusion of a ribbon rolling over the innermost roll (which comes to an end). With the same tool, cut up along the outside of the innermost roll. Now the ribbon appears to roll right up.

Fig. 4.12: With a 7-4mm, shape the innermost roll with push cuts (first done with an 11-6mm in Fig. 4.10). Round off the three outer sides of the inner roll with a flat tool. Use very sharp tools for this delicate work to keep the edge of the ribbon undamaged.

Carving a Piece of History

Note: Blow up drawing to 12 inches wide or 160% of original.

Fig. 4.13: The pattern is transferred to a 9-3/8" by 12" by 1" thick basswood board that has been fully prepared (planed, squared, and at the proper size and thickness). The board is firmly held in my vise for some heavy carving. I have sketched the background grey with a pencil to avoid any confusion while roughing out. I have also drawn a line around all four sides of the board, at about 1/2" deep, as a guide to how far down I should carve.

Fig. 4.14: I cut all the outlines of the pattern with a number 39-10mm V-tool (75 degrees). I have carved about 6 mm deep. The best method for making the V-tool cuts is to put the point of the tool right on the pencil line so you don't enlarge the design.

Note that I carved entirely from this vantage point. I switch from right to left hand carving as the grain dictates. (I am right-handed, so I prefer to hold the tool in my left hand and mallet in my right.) Throughout the carving of this panel, watch my hand and tool technique: tool in hand with my thumb going up the handle, wrist down on the carving, giving me complete control of the tool as to where and how far the blade will cut.

Fig. 4.15: The lowering of the background (the area sketched in pencil) is next. I am using a 7-20mm for the large areas and a 7-5mm or 12mm for the smaller areas. You can see the line I drew around the sides to guide how deep I carve. This picture also shows a perfect example of my hand and tool technique as described in Chapter 3.

Fig. 4.16: I now use an 11-7mm veiner to clean up around the outlines and go deeper into the wood. No V-tool cuts are used from this point on. Again, I never use stop cuts. I don't want to be limited to a sharp line. I have total control of the tool by putting my wrist down onto the wood. Without this kind of control, it would be easy for a razor sharp tool to go its own way, which could be dangerous to your carving, yourself, or both.

Fig. 4.17: The carving is mostly roughed out. You can see where the design is going, but there are no sharp outlines established yet. I don't want to say that this is the only way to approach a relief carving. Sometimes you have to hold to certain lines right from the beginning like in letter carving. Projects that are to stay precisely within the original design could be done with routers, especially with large-size projects. But, with this carving, we want the freedom to show our creative side. We want enough room to express this side through our hands.

Many of the outlines of this carving depend on the movement of the parts, with the ups and downs and curves that you want them to have. So outlining the areas of the leaves, stems, and ribbon, with a V-tool or a veiner (11 sweep) gives you enough room for the possibilities of free expression. You can enjoy the freedom of sculpting the end result. Using a router or your carving tools to cut to the exact line will not give you this freedom.

Fig. 4.18: Now I begin to sculpt the ribbon. I am lowering parts of it to give the feeling of movement—the unrolling of the ribbon as it crosses the panel. You could use a 7-12mm or a 5-12mm here and smooth the tool marks with a 3 sweep. I am resting my whole upper arm on the wood for comfort as well as tool control.

Fig. 4.19: As you can see, more sculpturing. Notice I moved all over the panel with a 7-12mm or 5mm and an 8-10mm to shape parts of the leaves, stems, and ribbon. Some of the leaves go down, and others go down and come up again or go under other parts like the ribbon. The stems have also been shaped so pointed parts push up, while other parts go down and even disappear behind leaves, other stems, and the ribbon. I want all the parts to flow in and amongst each another. Sculpturing like this brings life to the panel.

    Take a close look at the ribbon and you will see the stages of carving the linenfold developing right in front of you. Here is where you would be at a great advantage to have carved my linenfold exercises. If you would like a fast and easy way to make a model of the ribbon to have in front of you as you carve, cut a ribbon out of paper, roll it just as this one on the panel appears to be rolled, and tape it to your work bench. Now you have the real thing to look at as you carve it.

    The three leaves at the top left side of the panel (area in the dashed box of Fig. 4.19 and shown in close-up in Fig. 4.20) are carved in stages to show the steps I take to carve a leaf. Just start on the top left leaf and go counterclockwise. Notice each leaf is divided into three sections, and each section has two smaller points, one on each side. Then, at the base, where the stem comes in, there are two small round lobes, one on each side of the stem. Starting with the top left leaf, I have lowered the points of the three sections, each at a different height, with a 7-12mm. I have also cut in the three veins, which go up each section, with an 11-7mm.

4.20: On the bottom leaf, I enlarge the veins with an 8-10mm. The middle section has been dished going down and then up to rest on the ribbon.

On the third leaf I have dished out all three sections and shaped all the smaller points on both sides of each section with the 8-10mm. The three veins of the leaf have been carved back in with an 11-4mm. I also rounded the two lobes at the stem using a 4-12mm upside down (or a flat 12mm). The lobes are flat on top but rounded on the sides (not the same as the carving of grapes). The stem is rounded using a flat tool.

The outlines of the leaves have not been strictly defined yet. However, the three main sections are cupped (carved to go lower and then come back up again at the tip), all to different heights. The points on either side of each section have been similarly shaped, and the lobes on either side of the stem have been rounded. Also note the sections flow either left or right. Following the three leaves around starting from the leaf at the top left and going around counterclockwise, each leaf is a little more sculpted, and by the third leaf, it really comes alive!

Note the beginning of the stem on the far left. I have started putting a texture on it with the 5-12mm.

Fig. 4.21: I carve the general shape of the stems with a 5-12mm, or you can round over the stems with a flat tool. To give texture to the stems, use narrower (5-6mm) and deeper gouges (11-7mm and 4mm) or even the 39-10mm V-tool.

You can see two lines that were drawn on all four sides to guide in how deep I would carve the shaded areas (as mentioned in Fig. 4.13 & Fig. 4.15.). The second deeper line was drawn on too deep, so I drew a line at the proper depth and carved to it (1/2 inch deep). I ignored this deeper line and will sand it off after finishing the carving.

Fig. 4.22: Hollow out the end of the stems with an 11-6 or 7mm. To smooth out the top of the ribbon you can use a 3-20mm or even 12mm. However, I prefer a 2 1/2-20mm for these large surfaces. All the leaves are finished (as described in Fig. 4.19 & Fig. 4.20), and the grapes have been rounded with a 5-12mm (or 5-10mm) upside down. I have also started smoothing the background using a 2 1/2 sweep or 3 sweep, sized to fit the space.

Fig. 4.23: Here is another view of the nearly finished panel. Note the shapes of the finished leaves, grapes, and nearly finished stems and ribbon. You can see the effect of not carving to a strict outline. No two leaves are alike. Some sway left, some sway right, some are straight, and all are at different depths. They are very lifelike, and the stems look so natural. The background has been further smoothed with the flatter sweeps mentioned. Now, it is time to go back to the drawing and draw the pattern onto the carving using a soft lead pencil.

Fig. 4.24: The outline has been drawn back on the wood. Now that the sculpting has been finished, a defining line can be drawn around the scrolls, leaves, stems, and grapes.

Fig. 4.25: Now for the push cuts. I use several tools to fit the pencil line and give me a clean cut. Push cuts are not stop cuts. Here I am paring away very little wood; I'm not driving a tool deep into uncut wood and breaking wood fibers in every direction. The push cuts must be very clean to give a beautiful outline to the leaves, grapes, stems, and ribbon.

Note how I hold the tool for the push cuts. I am right-handed, so I hold the tool in my right hand and hold the metal part, the blade of the tool, with my left hand. The thumb and index finger of my left hand are clamping the blade while my other three fingers are folded into my hand. My left hand sits on the carving for control, while my right hand does all the maneuvering of the tool.

Finding a tool to fit every line would take a lot of tools, but that is not necessary. Select tools that will do the cleanest job possible. I have my favorites. You can go a long way with the tools you have. If you bought every tool every teacher told you to buy, you would have a lot of tools that you wouldn't use much. Keep to your favorites; use your tools wisely and do a clean job.

Fig. 4.26: The background has been cleaned up (with a 2 1/2-20mm, 12mm, and smaller) but is not completed. I am continuing on with the push cuts and am cutting right along the pencil line, cutting to meet the background cuts exactly. I use clean, precise cuts with very sharp tools. With the leaves cut to the line, they look more alive than ever.

Fig. 4.27: This is an excellent view of my left hand as described in Fig. 4.25. The grapes are not only getting push cuts but are also being rounded with the 5-12mm (10 and 8mm). No two grapes are exactly alike, so use the tools you have to make them different sizes and shapes. Also, note the linenfold before and after the line has been cut off. Before is not clean-cut and finished. After is just that, clean-cut and finished.

Fig. 4.28: Congratulations! You have just carved a beautiful panel, a duplicate of one carved in the 1600s! What a sense of accomplishment you must have! The finished work is even more beautiful than the very first time I saw this pattern. A beautiful woodcarving is always better than a plaster model.

My Personal Finish

This finish is one that I developed and have used for many years now. It protects the carving by sealing it well. I also like the contrast this finish adds and the overall warm glow it gives to the woodcarving.

Fig. 4.29: The carving is oiled with Watco clear finish. I want to seal the entire piece of wood, so I cover the front, back, and sides. I give it a day to be sure that it dries thoroughly. Without this initial sealing of the wood, the end grain would absorb more stain than the long grain. The woodcarving would stain unevenly and unpredictably.

After the Watco clear finish has dried, I apply Clear Briwax with a toothbrush to get into all the small areas of the woodcarving. Then I brush the Briwax out immediately after it is applied with a large natural bristle brush (like the one pictured in Fig. 4.33) that I use for clear wax only.

Fig. 4.30: Now I put Light Brown Briwax on with a toothbrush.

Fig. 4.31: Here you can see why I use a toothbrush. I can get into all the small areas of the carving.

Fig. 4.32: I am applying more Light Brown Briwax all over the panel. Note that the areas where I have applied the Briwax have been brushed out with a hard natural bristle brush (the left side of the picture). I don't wait until I have finished applying the wax to the whole panel. I brush it out every ten minutes after I apply it.

Fig. 4.33: All the Light Brown Briwax has been applied. Now is the time to vigorously brush over the entire panel to assure that the excess wax is removed.

Fig. 4.34: Now, I go over the entire panel with a soft nylon bristle brush.

Fig. 4.35: I follow up by polishing the woodcarving with a soft flannel cloth.

Fig. 4.36: I now polish it with a lint free cotton cloth, such as flannel.

Fig. 4.37: The finishing is done! The carving is uniformly stained, with a real nice contrast to it and a lovely satin glow.

Chapter 5
Letter Carving
Right and Wrong

Letter carving seems very difficult. To anyone untrained in carving letters, it is downright intimidating, especially if you spent a lot of time to get the Crest just right and now want to add words of wisdom, your initials, or the initials of the person (or people) you carved it for. Now, you may be terrified that you could make a mess out of your beautiful carving. Believe me when I tell you, letter carving is not that complicated!

A problem that my students bring up is they feel that they don't have near enough tools to cover all the curves and bends of one size of lettering, and there are so many letter sizes to cover. This again is not true. If you had to, you could carve letters in all sizes with as little as three tools. Using the method of incise letter carving I teach here, all you need is a good V-tool, a 3-12mm, and a curved tool such as a 5 sweep or a 7 sweep. So, you need not come to carving letters in wood with dread. In fact, I think you will come to enjoy letter carving once you start carving them the proper way.

I remember when I began carving letters. This is a tale from the dark side of woodcarving. I was carving in my father's studio and took on a job of my own. My father was on one side of the studio, and I was on the other side; both of us were carving away. The grain seemed the biggest obstacle. I started to carve and in no time I was quite irritated because I saw no way around it. I told my father in no uncertain terms my opinion that I would never get used to this. There was only silence from my dad's side of the studio. So, I continued to work with the V-tool, and I started to mellow out somewhat. The work in front of me was a real job, no practice cuts allowed. It had to be done with a mallet and since I am right-handed, when I switched to left-handed carving I had the mallet in my left hand. This was really awkward for me. When carving letters, as a beginner, you are thrown right into the middle of your weaknesses. But, I continued on until finally I started to get the concept. Remove the wood and then do the sides. My father said nothing because he knew I had the right tool, the V-tool, and just needed time to work out the process. By working this out myself, I never forgot the lesson.

When you look at an incised (one cut into the wood) letter drawn on the wood, you might want to take a tool and just stab it into the middle of the letter. You might want to drive your tools into the wood along the lines of the letter. But, you would do more damage than good. You have to learn some basic rules of carving.

Stabbing the tool into a flat piece of wood can cause enormous problems. By penetrating the wood with steel, straight in or at an angle, you cause the wood fibers to break open and loosen up in the most unpredictable ways. You can see in Fig. 5.1 how the fibers break out in about every direction and depth when stab cuts are used. You have lost control of the cut and this can only make things very hard to get back under control.

The best way to solve the problem of losing control is to not lose control from the beginning. Do not use stab cuts! Remove wood from the inside of the letter first before you start shaping the outline of the letter.

The V-Tool

Now we are going to carve an incised letter that has some curves. As I said, letter carving does not take a lot of tool shapes to match letter shapes. However, the parting tool (the V-tool) is essential for relief carving and especially for incised letter carving. Therefore, you should be very particular as to which one you buy.

The V-tools you should consider buying are the 39 75 degree V-tool (the angle inside the V of the V-tool is 75 degrees) and the 41 60 degree V-tool. These tools, with a width of 8 or 10mm, are very useful.

The 90-degree (or 100-degree) V-tool is one I would never purchase because, as a professional carver for 68 years, I have never had any use for one. The same goes for the 50 Macaroni, which is shaped like the bottom of a box, a flat bottom and two opposite sides at 90 degrees to the bottom. Some say it is two V-tools in one. I say it is a waste of money. Last but not least is the 49 winged V-tool, which looks like a V-tool with curved sides. The problem with these tools is, no matter in which direction you carve, there is always one side that goes against the grain of the wood. That is, unless you are going with the grain. The practical use for these tools is very limited. These odd shapes would make a mess of the other side of the grain.

For regular use of a V-tool, I always start with a 39 75 degree V-tool in the 10mm size. It is 10mm from the top of one wing to the other. You can make the tiniest cuts with the 10mm, so don't worry that almost every Beginner's Set seems to have a 39 6mm. The 10mm can do all that work and more. The 41 60 degree V-tool is good to define or accent carvings in certain places. Don't make a sharp curved cut in hardwood with a 60 degree tool. Small pieces of the hardwood, like oak, get stuck in the tool and can break chips out that you don't want out. This has happened to me several times over the years.

Use the 39 75 degree V-tool as a starting tool on a project. It is important to sharpen the blade of the tool to the proper angle. Sharpening the blade to an 18 degree bevel is ideal for V-tools. However, when you make it too short (say a 30 degree bevel) you have to apply too much power to cut through the wood and, consequently, you have to hold the tool almost straight up to get it to cut. Also, where the two sides of the V-tool come together, there should be a sharp V, not a U. The sharper the V, the better the V-tool is. Yes, the inside and the outside must match. Needless to say, some manufacturers have better V-tools than others. When only the outside is rounded, I take the tool to a belt sander with 100 grit sandpaper on it. Then, I carefully make the bottom sharp. A sharp V-tool is a very useful V-tool.

In lettering, the V-tool does a lot of work. I would practice with this tool for a while. Cut short curves with the mallet. Just do real light tapping with the mallet to move the V-tool in short, controlled movements. Do this with your left hand and your right hand. Always make the cuts in curves less deep than in the straight cuts so no break-outs in the wood occur. Always go for your V-tool first. Don't use stab cuts ever.

Now, let's move on with letter carving. If you want to see me actually carving letters, you may purchase my DVD called *Letter Carving with Nora Hall* at www.norahall.com.

Fig. 5.1 shows an example of stabbing the wood at an angle with a flat tool. If the two lines represented the two sides of the letter L, you would be stabbing in on one side and then the other, trying hard to make sure you don't destroy either side of the letter. That is a lot of work and a waste of time just to remove wood from the inside of the letter. Again, do not use stab cuts and lose control from the beginning.

Fig. 5.2 Let's try the proper way to remove the wood between two lines that represent part of a letter. Fig. 5.2 shows how a V-tool will cut between the two lines. Notice that the cut goes in and cuts between the lines with total control.

Fig. 5.3 shows me cleaning up that cut with the V-tool, making a nice V cut right in the center of the two lines. In the photos I have the V cuts come right up to the stab cuts so you can see the difference and how easily I took control of my cuts.

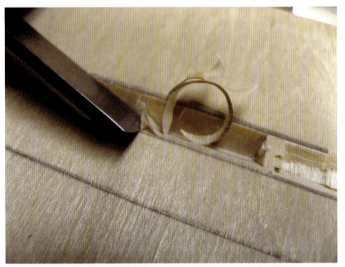

In Fig. 5.4, I use a 3-12 mm to smooth out the sides up to the pencil line. I keep the 3-12mm in place and move it back and forth until I get a clean cut and a shine on the side of the letter. I use a 3 sweep in place of a 1 (or flat tool). The 3 sweep creates a better shadow than a flat tool and makes a sharper outline so the letter looks better to the observer. Let's stay with the proper way.

The Letter L

Since we have covered how to properly carve a letter and have dealt with the area between two lines, let's carve the letter L. The horizontal leg of this letter goes right with the grain, and the vertical leg goes straight against the grain. I would recommend a very sharp V-tool. I always recommend carving with the sharpest tools possible.

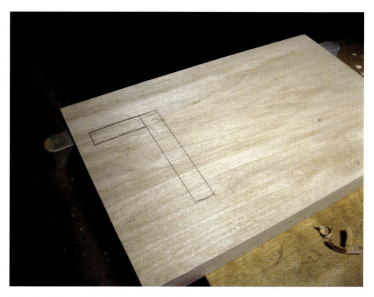

Fig. 5.5: First, the letter is copied onto the wood. A pattern for this exercise is located in Appendix B.

Fig. 5.6: Using a 39-10mm 75 degree V-tool, I make five miter cuts, one in each outside corner. The cut starts shallow and goes down to about 4-5mm deep, going in at about a 45 degree angle.

Fig. 5.7: Using the same V-tool, I cut out a substantial amount of wood. I put the sharp bottom of the V in the center of the two lines that make up this letter and drive the tool with a mallet.

Fig. 5.8: Now, I make the same deep cut down the center of the other length of this letter. Also, notice my tool hand in the last two pictures, wrist down to have full control of how far, how deep, and where the tool can move. Now, in this picture, you can see my tool hand with the wrist down on the carving, my thumb going up the handle, my fingers wrapped around the tool, and a mallet in the other hand being used to move the tool. This is comfortable, safe, and very accurate.

Fig. 5.9: Use a 3-12mm down on the wood so the blade of the tool cuts into the side of the letter. Keep the 3-12mm on the wood, making very short cuts and slowly sliding the tool back and forth. Keep this up until you have widened the angle from the bottom of the letter (cut by the V-tool) to the pencil line that marks the sides of the letter. Now, you have a perfectly carved side. The secret here is to keep the tool on the wood, cutting and sliding it back and forth, burnishing the wood with the metal blade. This will give you a clean cut and polish the surface of the side of the letter at the same time.

Fig. 5.10: You can see that the two sides are done. Now, it is time to do the ends. I do the ends between the 2 miter cuts with the 3-12mm. Remember, you want that slight concave side that the 3 sweep creates, which gives some shadow that the flat tool does not. Overall, the letter stands out better.

Fig. 5.11: Now I use a 41-10mm 60 degree V-tool to shape up the bottom V where the two sides come together. Since the two sides of the V-tool are closer together, I can do this detailing without worry of hitting the side of the letter. If you don't have a 41, then use your 39 with care. I lightly cut up the stem of the letter to define the original V shape of the letter and make the bottom nice and crisp.

Fig. 5.12: I don't remove a lot of wood, just enough to make a nice line along the bottom. You can also see those corner cuts I made in Fig. 5.6 and how nicely they shape the end of the letter. I retouched them up, also, using the 41-10mm 60 degree V-tool.

The Letter J

If your letter J doesn't look quite right, then carve it again while the idea is fresh in your mind. I can't think of a faster way to learn than by repetition. As I said at the very beginning of this chapter, at the point when I was learning how to carve letters, I became frustrated when I couldn't get the tool to work the way I wanted, and it was a real job. But, after so much repetition, I could make those cuts with perfection. I went from a beginner to an expert after about one full day.

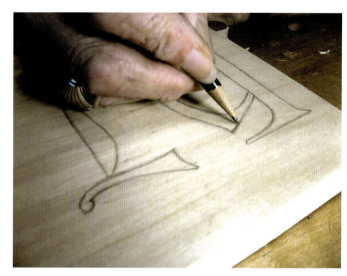

Fig. 5.13: After I have transferred the letters onto the wood with copy paper, I go over them with a soft pencil to make my lines clear.

Fig. 5.14: Now, it's time to carve the second letter in from the left, the letter J.

Fig. 5.15: With the wood firmly held on my carving bench, I pick up my mallet and start clearing wood with my 39-10mm 75 degree V-tool, which is totally in my control (my wrist is down on the wood).

Fig. 5.16: Ah, the sweet sound of a razor-sharp tool slicing through the wood!

Fig. 5.17: In the two corners at the top of the J, I start with two miter cuts, just as I did with the letter L. These cuts will assure that the V-cut, which I will follow up with, does not just run with the grain and break through the pencil line.

Fig. 5.18: Now I make the big cut right up the center and to the miter cuts.

51

Fig. 5.19: The rough cut is finished. Notice how the depth of the cut decreases as the width of the letter stroke narrows.

Fig. 5.20: Going around the curve at the bottom of the letter, I follow my own advice and cut a little shallower. I'm tapping lightly on the mallet. If one side of the curve is breaking out too much, then turn the tool around and go the other way. I watch the grain carefully. Go slowly and watch for too much break out.

Fig. 5.21: Here, I am widening the straight part of the letter J with a 3-12mm.

Fig. 5.22: I made two miter cuts in the very top end of the letter (Fig. 5.17). Here, you can see how I use a 3-12mm and 3-4mm to make a short cut between the miter cuts to form that end of the letter.

Fig. 5.23: Now I can finish the shaping of that end, cutting only to reach the miter cuts.

Fig. 5.24: I am now finishing the major part of the top of the letter with the 3-12mm. Cut with the tool down and at an angle from the bottom made by the V-tool to the pencil lines and go right up to the miter cuts. Remember to keep the tool in place and move it back and forth to burnish the side and leave a nice clean and polished end of the letter like we did on the letter L.

Fig. 5.25: I am widening the other side of the vertical part of the letter. It bulges out, so I switch to a 5-20mm and carefully carve up, then down the side, so as not to break out any wood. Keep the tool on an angle from the pencil line to the V-tool cut.

Fig. 5.26: I cut this wide section very carefully and at an angle that reaches the bottom.

Fig. 5.27: The 5-20mm fits the line perfectly, so I use it to make push cuts from the pencil line down to the V-tool cut.

Fig. 5.28: This picture shows you what to do if you don't have a tool that exactly fits the pencil line of the letter. Take your closest tool, say a 4-12mm, and use just part of the cutting edge to follow that line around.

Fig. 5.29: Back to cutting sideways again... I use the 5-20mm, (3-12mm, 4, 5 sweep, etc.) until I have removed the wood where the bulge of the letter is.

Fig. 5.30: Then, I switch to my 3-12mm to cut into and along the side of the letter to finish it. The 5 sweep* would make the side too hollow. Remember, we only want a light concave to create a shadow that makes the letter stand out. In this picture, you can see the work done by the 5-20mm cutting down to widen the vertical part of the letter. (*5 sweep refers to the depth of the gouge. Refer to Appendix A for tool shape identification.)

Fig. 5.31: We have the 3-12mm, down on its side, finishing the side of the letter from the pencil line to the center cut of the V-tool.

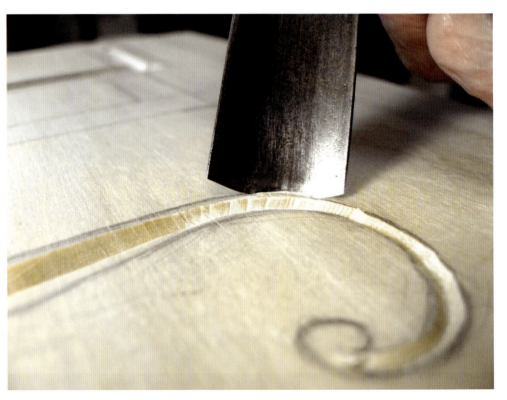

Fig. 5.32: The 5-20mm fits pretty well in this part of the curve. Use caution and cut down at the angle set in by the V-tool.

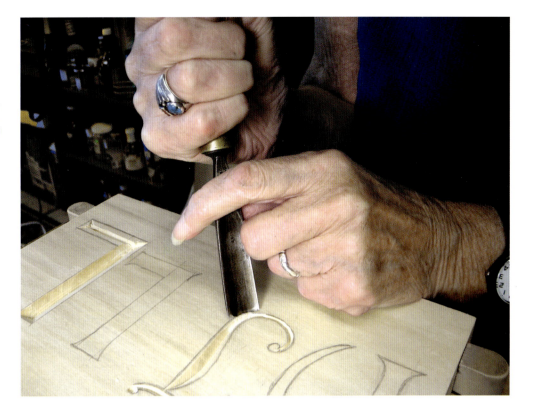

Fig. 5.33: The curve of the letter is getting too tight for the 5 sweep to fit. Use a deeper tool, if you have one, to get around this bottom curl of the letter. I have switched to a 6 sweep.

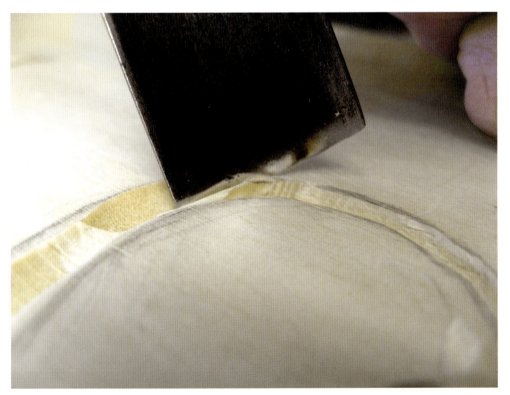

Fig. 5.34: With this technique, I use part of the 5 sweep's blade to cut the curved side smooth. If you don't have a sweep that fits the curve, then use this method. Very few carvers own all the tools necessary to fit every part, size or shape of all letters, but we can still get this side cut smooth.

Fig. 5.35: I found a tool that is a little too deep, but it will do an excellent job.

Fig. 5.36: I have a tool that is a close fit, and I am carefully working with the grain to get this side smooth.

Fig. 5.37: Progress! Remember not to carve when you're tired or frustrated with your work or progress. The carving will wait until another day, and you'll be glad you waited.

Fig. 5.38: Now, I'm on the other side working with the grain and using a 3-12mm to get that perfect curve in the letter wall.

Fig. 5.39: I continue with the 3-12mm. Remember, the tool is held against the side of the letter and moved back and forth to polish and clean cut the side.

Fig. 5.40: Now, I need to carve with the 11-6mm.

Fig. 5.41: I use the 11-6mm to cut the incised pearl that is at one end of the top of the letter.

Fig. 5.42: Now, I cut the incised pearl at the bottom of the letter. What an interesting ending for these parts of the letter!

Fig. 5.43: Notice the hand grip I use. Blade in my left hand to hold the tool in place, handle in my right to manipulate the tool. Believe me when I say that after you get these tool holds down, you will carve faster and more accurately than ever before.

Fig. 5.44: I finish the letter with my 41-10mm 60 degree V-tool by making the bottom nice and clean and giving it a sharp V. These final clean up cuts are delicate and do not take off much wood. But now that you look at the letter, you can see the extra shadow brought out by making the sides with a slightly curved tool (the 3-12mm).

Fig. 5.45: You have just carved a beautiful version of the letter J. Congratulations! Yes, it may have seemed complicated, and, by just reading the instructions, you may have gotten the impression that it takes forever to carve. This is far from true. I can cut a J out very quickly. It just takes time to explain, so please get carving. If you have been carving along with the book, then you are probably starting to understand the time-tested method of removing wood and then shaping the carving and burnishing the wood clean and polished. It is a method that has been handed down for generations.

Lettering B and S

Now, I will carve the letter B. You probably have the routine down so well, you can do it in your sleep.

A.) We tape the pattern to the wood. Next, we slip a piece of carbon paper between the wood and the pattern. Then, I like to go over the lines with a soft pencil (a #2 pencil will do just fine).

B.) Make miter cuts in all corners in the letter like we did with the letter L.

C.) Remove the wood inside the letter by using a 39-10mm 75 degree V-tool right in the center of the two lines that make up the sides of the letter.

D.) Then, choose tools that are the closest to the curve of the line and cut down at an angle from the pencil line to the bottom of the V-tool cut.

E.) Place the 3-12mm down on the wood and cut the side of the letter wall to give it a little curve and thus a shadow.

F.) Clean up the bottom V cut with a slightly smaller-angled (narrower) V-tool (the 41-10mm).

Now for carving B and S:

Figs. 5.46 & 5.47: With the letters traced on my wood and the wood clamped securely on my bench, I cut right through the centers of the S and B and make miter cuts on the B with my 39-10 V-tool. A pattern for this exercise is located in Appendix B. (above and opposite page top)

Fig. 5.48: I am now going right through the center of the letter B to remove that wood with a 39-10mm V-tool.

Fig. 5.49: Carve carefully around the curves. If the curve is too tight, the wood will break out. My hand is on the wood, and I slowly move the tool around the upper part of the B. I am in total control.

Fig. 5.50: I must also be very careful to follow the grain. Also, notice that when the curve gets tighter, I cut shallower.

Fig. 5.51: I am carving the S with my 39-10mm V-tool.

Fig. 5.52: Using the tool I have that closely fits the curve, I cut down at an angle to meet the V-tool cut. I am using a 5-20mm.

Fig. 5.53: Here I use only part of the tool's blade because that is all that fits this curve.

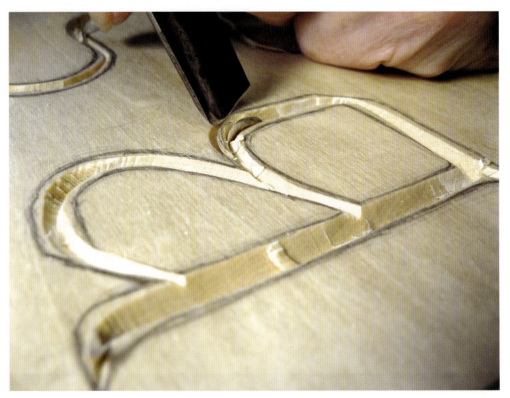

Fig. 5.54: Here I am fitting the curves of the B as best as I can. On the tighter curves, I use a deeper gouge that is also smaller in width.

Fig. 5.55: Using the same tool, I cut one side of the letter curve with one side of my tool, and the other side of the curve with the outside of my tool. I cut the concave side with this tool, and then I cut the convex side with the opposite side of the same tool.

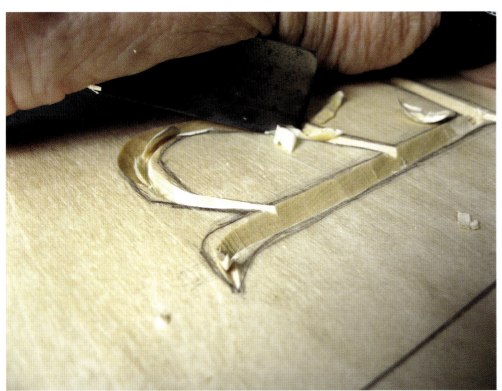

Fig. 5.56: With the 3-12 down on the wood, I cut the finished side with that slight curve of the 3 sweep to give the letter more shadow.

Fig. 5.57: I continue on with the 3-12mm, and, by now, you can see the advantage of carving the side of a letter this way rather than with a flat tool. The letters really stand out better.

Fig. 5.58: Watch the grain and take your time with the 3-12mm.

Fig. 5.59: I am making a nice long controlled cut with the 3-12mm down on the wood, cutting the side from the pencil line to the bottom of the V cut. I keep the tool on the wood and push it back and forth to burnish the wood smooth while shaping it.

Fig. 5.60: Now, I am cleaning up the bottom of the letter with a narrower V-tool, the 41-10mm 60 degree V-tool.

Fig. 5.61: The letter B is finished while the letter S is showing different stages of completion. The letter S shows a nice contrast between the beginning stage where I have removed wood from between the lines and a later stage, which is in the process of being finished.

I believe you now have the framework to carve any letter you would like. You know the steps and you know how to make your letters stand out. It is amazing what a little extra shadow will do for a letter. By now, you have hopefully done enough examples to know that you don't need a room full of tools to do all shapes and sizes of letters.

This method of carving letters avoids broken or damaged wood (no stab cuts). There are no angles to measure or worry about. You just carve from inside the pencil line down to the V-tool cut that is right in the center of the lines that make up the sides of the letters. And no more letters with flat sides. This method, taught for centuries by the Old World masters, makes letter carving much easier to learn. I believe that if you have carved this far, you will find letter carving enjoyable. I bet you didn't see that coming. So, use fewer tools and carve better letters.

Chapter 6
Carving the Crest
Introduction

I am going to show you how to carve this Crest (Fig. 6.1), or Cartouche as it is known to architects and the like. A Cartouche is an ornate or ornamental frame, usually an oval surrounded by scrolls and such. It was at its prime in the Renaissance period. As you can see, this Crest is framed by scrolls, pearls (or peas in a pod, as I see them), and lily leaves that bend and curve in a very lifelike way. The center of the Crest is higher in the middle and goes deeper towards the frame, so I often refer to this enclosed area as pillow-shaped. Outside the frame, the background is flat.

I carve full-time and was able to finish this carving in about one day. For less experienced carvers, it will take longer, perhaps a few days. For those of you who carve part-time, whenever you can, this carving will take longer, perhaps much longer, but do not get discouraged. The thrill of seeing the parts come into shape is well worth the effort and time. This carving can be done in about any size. This one will be on a piece of wood 6" tall by 11" wide by 1-3/4" thick. Imagine a small crest for a jewelry box or a large one for words of wisdom. The size and use is almost infinite.

For wood I used Basswood. The grain is nice and tight, and the wood is a joy to carve. It is also very light and even in color, so the carving really stands out. You don't want the wild grain of a burl to compete with the Crest or the wording. I suppose Cherry or Maple could be used, but Cherry is dark and both woods are so hard. Sugar pine or White pine are light in color but tend to splinter too much.

Watch my hands during this project. I have the tool held in my hand with my wrist resting on the carving itself. This gives me perfect control over how far my tool can travel. This is very important. If I push the tool with the other hand or use a mallet, the cutting edge of the tool cannot go out of control. I don't have to worry about cutting something off that should have stayed on. By resting the tool hand down, I am in complete control of the cut and the cutting edge. Besides, I can carve away in comfort. I never scoop out large amounts of wood, even when taking out the background. I let the tool do the work. As you can see from my beginning cuts with the V-tool, I rest my hand on the carving and move the tool along, rarely taking the tool from the wood (which really speeds up my carving time) and cutting at the same depth as I move around the carving.

To teach you how to carve the Crest, I will first teach you how to carve the individual parts of the frame. These scrolls, pearls, sea shells, and lily leaves are things you need to know how to carve well, because they keep reappearing in various ways or in various combinations in European relief carving. If you can carve them well, you will have a strong foundation and will become more proficient, and totally independent, at this style of relief carving. You will know how to approach a complex carving, break it down, and carve it well. Nothing will seem too hard. You can say "I can carve!" with conviction. You will know how to carve.

Learning to carve the parts well is also essential to carving this Crest. The Crest will be our first application of putting the parts together. You will master the control of your tools and know how to carve these parts in various wood grain directions. This is where you master the wood grain, and it is very important.

Now we will carve the four main parts of the frame: pearls and the sea shell, lily leaves, the bottom scrolls, and the scrolls at the top. To do these exercises you will need a board of basswood (10" wide by 2' long and 3/4" thick).

Now, let's carve the details until we can do them well.

The Pearls and the Shell

Note that as I carve with the V-tool, there are times when I cut right across the grain and times where I cut at a slight diagonal to the grain. Cutting at a slight diagonal means one side of the cut will break the grain of the wood, leaving a jagged edge, and the other side of the cut will be clean. I make sure my clean cuts are on the side of my woodcarving project. If I need both sides to be clean-cut while cutting on a diagonal, then I cut very shallow and use push cuts to get where I need to be. The pearls or "peas in a pod" are good examples of that here.

You will have to carve left-handed and right-handed. This may seem difficult at first, but you will quickly become accustomed to it. You will also learn how to work the grain of the wood. Soon you won't have to even think about where the smooth side of the grain will be. You will just make the proper cuts with the carving side smooth and the other side coarse. All it takes is practice. Keep practicing the proper method, and soon the method will be second nature. This is not a time to pick up poor technique.

Fig. 6.2: We have transferred the image of the left side of the Crest onto the wood, using carbon paper. The side is transferred exactly the way it appears on our finished carving. The row of pearls (or peas in a pod) and the parts of a shell run perpendicular to the grain of the wood. The image is the same size as the one for our finished carving.

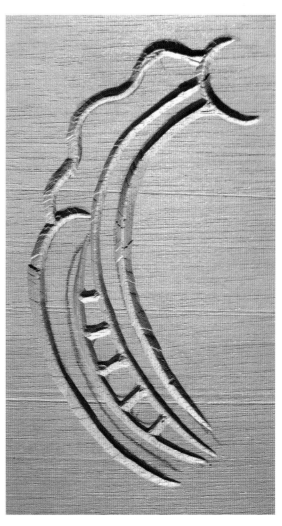

Fig. 6.3: Using the 39-10mm V-tool, I have carefully cut in most of the lines. You can see that I didn't cut along the line next to the pearls.

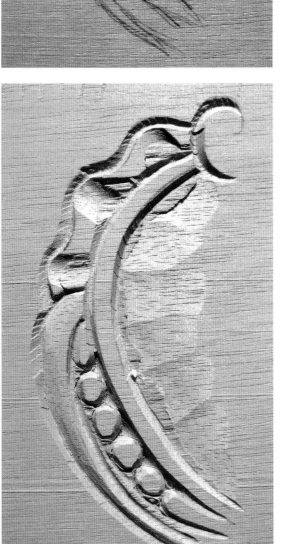

Fig. 6.4: We begin to shape the inside surface of the Crest, which is high in the center and lower around the sides (a pillow-shaped center) using a 4 or 5-12mm. The pearls are being shaped with light push cuts, using a 5-6mm. We shape the shell by using a 9-10mm to make 3 deep cuts which create the beginning of the wave motion. Connect the deep cuts by flipping the 3-12mm over and using the inside to add to the wave motion.

Now is the time to shape the line next to the row of pearls (peas) that we didn't cut with the V-tool in the beginning. We now cut along that line with an 11-6mm. (Notice how it looks like a pea pod.)

The peas are rounded off and given perfect outlines with a 5-6mm. Clean up the little corners in between them with a 3-4mm. Use the same tools and the 11-6mm on the upper part of the "pea pod" to give it shape and clean it up. Clean up the V-tool cut at the very top, and also round the back of the pea pod with a 5-6mm. The back of the shell is cleaned up with the 8-6mm and the 5-6mm.

The area between the inside of the crest (the pillow-shaped area) and the entire side (peas, shells and all) has a very clean "U" shaped area. We have left the space for it. Now, using the 11-6mm, carefully carve with the grain to give a nice, clean, and beautiful transition. Here would be a good time to review how to get clean cuts across the grain as I wrote it in the text following Fig. 6.3. Actually, I hope by now you understand how to carve cross grain. If you don't, then with a little more practice you will.

Now you can see how the shell was shaped. On the pillow side of the shell, there are three concave cuts with a 9-10mm connected by two shallow convex shapes cut by the 3-12mm. The inside of the concave cuts were finished with 11-4mm cuts. I used a 3 or 5 sweep to fit and slightly undercut the U cut in front of the shell. On the back side I used an 8-6mm and a 5-6mm to give a slight undercut to the back and a nice clean cut.

Fig. 6.5: We smooth the inside of the Crest with a 3-16mm or 3-12mm (note the pillow shape, high in the center and lower around the sides). The upper edge of the shell is cut in with an 8-6mm to emphasize the wavy edge. The back of these shell waves are undercut to create more dimension with the same tool.

The Lily Leaves

Fig. 6.6: The lily leaves are copied on a piece of basswood, the same size as they will be on the finished project, and oriented with the grain the same way they will be on the finished project. To make any or all the lily leaves easier to visualize, you can make a quick life-size model of any leaf. Just cut out a piece of paper the same width and length and fold the paper to match the leaf you are having problems with. Now tape it to your work bench. You now have a life-size model to look at and work with. This little trick of making a quick and easy model helped me a lot when I started carving linenfold and ribbons, too.

Fig. 6.7: Using the 39-10mm V-tool, I carve the outline of the leaves as usual, about 4 mm deep, putting the tip of the V-tool on the line of the pattern so as not to enlarge the leaves. However, I do not cut the two little lines that come across the leaves. I will carve those later with a different tool.

Fig. 6.8: I now carve those two little lines left from the pattern. Using an 11-4mm, I start at the bottom and go through the center of the small, lower portion of the leaf to give the illusion that the small part of the leaf is curling. The top leaf is cut, also from the bottom, on an angle just along the line. These cuts are essential to make the leaves appear to curve over the rest of the leaf.

Fig. 6.9: We see clearly the bottom of the top leaf is tilted down and disappears under the tip of the leaf which folds over it. By tilting this last short point to the left and rounding it at the fold, we use a simple technique for carving ribbons or for folding cloth. The bottom leaf curls down and comes out underneath, slightly curling up. You should tilt this leaf, also, but in the opposite direction as the one above it. Undercut with the 11-4mm. To tilt the blades of the lily leaves and to give a delicate shape to their surface, I used a 5-12mm or 14mm. I used the same tool (and a 5-6mm where necessary) to cut into the sides of the leaves and to make them appear to come up some and to accent the folds.

The Top Scrolls

Fig. 6.10: A piece of carbon paper, the full size pattern, and a piece of wood oriented just as the scroll will be on the Crest is needed for this exercise. The grain of the wood runs the length of the scroll. Two of the lines on this pattern are stippled so they will not be outlined with the V-tool, but they indicate an area where concave cuts will be made. The pattern for the crest is on page 75.

Fig. 6.11: We outline the pattern with our 39-10mm V-tool. Watch the ever changing grain while doing these cuts.

Fig. 6.12: Use an 11-6mm (or 10-6mm) to make the concave cuts along the stippled lines. The cuts run into their individual scrolls. Where those cuts stop, you start cutting with a 5-6mm or 3-6mm, doing push cuts around to the scroll ends.

Fig. 6.13: Now we take the tools we have used and clean up all the cuts including the 5-6mm used to clean up the outer V-tool cut line. Also, use an 11-4 cut to decorate the leaf part of this design (the small "U" cut on top).

Now, one more detail and the Crest will seem easy (or at least easier).

The Bottom Scrolls

Fig. 6.14: Again, the pattern of the full size scroll is transferred to wood using carbon paper. The wood is oriented just as the scroll will be on the Crest. The grain should run the length of the scroll.

Fig. 6.15: With the 39-10mm V-tool, I cut out the outline. I drew in two stippled lines, one on the top left and one on the bottom right going into the scroll. Don't touch those with the V-tool. We will deal with those areas later.

Fig. 6.16: Using an 11-6mm (or 10-6mm), carve along the stippled line at the top of the stylized acanthus leaf for a concave area. I also cut into and up the side of the scroll on the right with the same tool (the second stippled line). Next, I finish the scroll on the other side, using a 5-6mm to cut around it and then a 3-6mm (or a flat tool) to clean it up. I use these same tools (the 5-6mm and then the 3-6mm or a flat tool) to round the acanthus leaf parts all around.

Fig. 6.17: Using an 11-4mm, I finish the line that goes into the acanthus leaf (first seen cut on Fig. 6.15). I make two small decorative cuts in the middle of the leaf with an 11-4mm. I make each decorative cut with a downward cut and then a sideways cut. Next, I use the same tool making a teardrop shape, and then I follow the deep cut all the way out of the leaf to separate the two parts of the leaf. The rest of the veins of the leaf are cut with the same tool, the 11-4mm.

Now, using the tools at hand, we go about cleaning all the cuts for a beautiful scroll with acanthus leaves. We go around the carving with the 5-6mm and the 3-6mm to clean up all the chatter cuts left by the V-tool. We use the 11-6mm (or 10-6mm) to make the concave cuts very clean until you have a nice, clean bottom of the Crest scroll that you can be proud of.

Congratulations! You have carved almost every aspect of the Crest carving! You should now be ready to carve the Crest as a whole. Remember, the Crest (or Cartouche for the architects in the crowd) has a pillow-shaped inside. It rises in the center and drops down to the sides all around. Outside the frame, the background is flat.

The carving should be a lot easier for you now that you know the straightforward approach I always take when carving a piece, or part of the whole.

1.) Always orient the practice carving on the wood so the grain runs the same way as it will on the finished carving.

2.) Outline with the V-tool.

3.) Use the tools you have (if you have a tool that is close, use it!) to roughly form the part being carved.

4.) Never use stab cuts!

Carving the Crest Step by Step

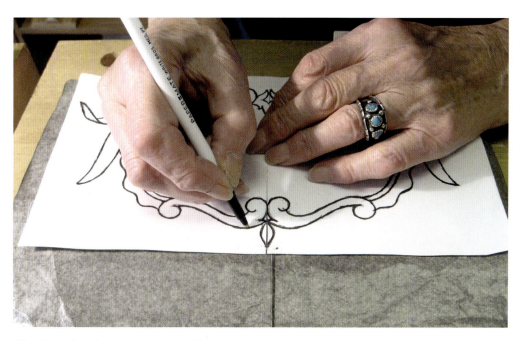

Fig. 6.18: Starting with a piece of Basswood 6"W by 11"L by 1 3/4"T (the grain runs the length), I have carefully placed the pattern on the wood and then placed carbon paper under that. Now, I trace the lines of the pattern with a ball point pen.

Fig. 6.19: Take the pattern off, and the image of the Crest is on the wood.

Fig. 6.20: I draw a line around the four sides of the wood, 1/2 the way down, so I know how deep I can carve. With this done, we can secure the wood to the bench and begin to carve.

Fig. 6.21: Using my 39-10mm V-tool (6mm, 8mm, whatever you have), I carefully outline the pattern, cutting about 4mm deep. Keep the V-tool right on the line so as not to enlarge the pattern. You can see my hand resting on the carving giving me complete control of the carving tool. Complete control is the key here.

Fig. 6.22: As you can see, I make controlled cuts and watch the grain to avoid chipping wood out that I don't want out. Then, I move my tool along the pattern line to make more controlled cuts. I try to move quickly along the pattern lines without picking up the V-tool. This way I always have the tool in the correct position to carve and can move right along. This really helps to carve faster, and, as you can imagine, saves time. I also try to make as many right-handed cuts as I can before shifting to the left-handed cuts. This is a very efficient way to carve.

Fig. 6.23: With the V cuts finished, I begin to remove the background with a 7-20mm or 12mm and a mallet. We will take the background down around the crest. I go close to the center line depth, drawn all around the sides of the piece of wood, but I don't worry about smoothing it out now.

Hopefully, after all those exercises, you can switch from right- to left-hand carving (both with and without the mallet), without thinking too much about it. As pointed out earlier, you need to be able to change hands as you carve because the grain changes. This is a good carving for you to learn this on. In the classes I teach, the students begin to find they don't even notice the difference of changing from right to left-handed carving after about an hour's work. You may not think so at first, but by the time you finish this carving, changing from your right to left hand will have become second nature.

Fig. 6.24: I am beginning to lower one side of the inside of the crest with a 7-20mm. The inside of the crest rises in the center but goes down around the sides. It is pillow-shaped. Again, wrist on the wood, tool in my hand with my thumb going up the handle, fingers around the blade of the tool, I am in complete control. This kind of control is crucial to carving successfully (no slipping and taking off part of your carving or yourself) and it is a comfortable way to carve.

Fig. 6.25. I'm working all around the center mound of the inside of the crest using a 7-20mm. I have perfect control of the tool hand while carving. No slips here. You can see that as I worked around the inside of the crest, I have had my hand planted and could only carve so far. Nowhere is that easier to see than in this photo. All the tool cuts around the inside of the crest are the same length. I plant my hand and carve towards the side to make the sides deeper. Then, I rotate my hand and do the same cut over again and then again: Perfect control with or without the mallet.

Fig. 6.26: Now, I use the 39-10mm V-tool again to clean up and make the first V-tool cut a little deeper and sharper.

Fig. 6.27: With a 2 1/2 -20mm or 3-20mm, I smooth and shape the inside of the crest to a finer degree. Remember, the inside of the crest has a pillow shape; it's higher in the center.

Fig. 6.28: Again, I am making the inside of the crest smoother with the 2 1/2 or 3 sweep. In this close-up shot you can clearly see how I used the V-tool to cut deeper and cleaner. Now I use the 2 1/2 (or 3) 20mm to get the sides deeper to match.

Fig. 6.29: Here I am using the 2 1/2 (or 3) 20mm to shape the inside of the crest for a nice, clean, and well defined surface. I am taking off less wood, doing light push cuts to get the inside pillow shape right. To get the cleanest inside bottom surface, I could use the 1-16mm, but that will come with the finishing cuts.

Fig. 6.30: Here is a close up of that finishing cut using the 1-16mm. You can see how beautiful the pillow shape of the crest has become. You can also see the light cuts I made between each pearl with the V-tool and the space I left for the U shape I make along the interior sides.

Fig. 6.31: I carved a nice U shape all along the side of the crest wall with an 11-6mm. Watch the grain! You are carving across the grain and need to be careful to change from right to left-handed carving. I am beginning to shape the pearls (or peas in a pod), round with the inside of my 5-6mm using push cuts with care.

Push cuts are cuts that pare off small amounts of wood until you get the right shape and a clean line. Being right-handed, I hold the tool in my right hand and I hold the metal part of the tool, the blade, between the thumb and index finger of my left hand. The other three fingers of my left hand fold into my left palm. I want my left hand on the carving for control, and I maneuver the tool with my right hand. I pick the tool that fits the curve of the cut as close as possible.

Fig. 6.32: We are getting there. The U cut all along the side of the crest is perfectly shaped with the 11-6mm. I will undercut along the top of it later. The peas in a pod are shaped and the U shape that makes up the top of the pod is cleanly cut in with the 11-6mm. The peas will now be well-defined.

Fig. 6.33: I cut the small areas between the peas with a 3-4mm, using push cuts to get a nice clean carving.

Fig. 6.34: Now you can see how the peas clean up (before and after) using the 5-6mm to push cut them into shape and the 3-4mm to get into the deep corners and spaces to make nice clean peas in a pod.

Fig. 6.35: Using just part of the blade of a flat chisel (1-16mm), I clean-up the inside surface very close to the acanthus leaf portion of one of the two scrolls at the bottom of the crest.

Fig. 6.36: Use push cuts with the 5-6mm to clean up the area where the acanthus leaf portion of this scroll contacts the inside bottom of the crest.

Fig. 6.37: To shape the shell, make three deep cuts with a 9-12mm. Then, connect the three deep cuts with shallow cuts from the inside of the blade of a 3-12mm, thus making the cuts slightly convex.

Fig. 6.38: Slight undercutting of the shell from the back gives it a more three-dimensional look, so undercut the back using a 9-12mm (or an 8-10mm) and a 3-12mm (or 4-12mm).

Fig. 6.39: I undercut the U shape I made with an 11-6mm in Fig. 6.32, that is between the shell and the inside of the crest. I make push cuts with a 7-6mm all along the back side of that U shape. I want to make that transition from shell to U shape as clean as possible. Then, I go along the shell and cut veins from the top of the shell downward to the undercut of the U with an 11-4mm and 2mm, curving the cuts some as I cut down.

Fig. 6.40: Here I cut down on an angle with the 11-4mm to begin the shape of the lily leaf.

Fig. 6.41: Now, I undercut the top of that lily leaf with the 11-4mm. It may appear that I am jumping around on this carving. I have carved so many of these crests that while I was in that position and had the tool in my hand, I just made the cuts on the end of that lily leaf, one more part carved and with no extra work.

Fig. 6.42: Now, I start to shape the scrolls at the top of the crest. I start by rounding the ends with push cuts using an inverted 5-12mm and a 4-12mm. The surface on the inside of the Crest has been described as pillow-shaped. It rises in the center and goes down around the sides. You can really see that in these two photos (Figs. 6.42 and 6.43). The original pattern lines are still on the center of the pillow.

Fig. 6.43: I am making the finish push cuts with a 5-6mm (or a tool to fit) to clean up around the round end of the scroll where it meets the inside surface of the crest. Two scrolls come together on the top of the crest. Both scrolls are carved the same way, so I will only describe one. Start by cutting to the round scroll ends with an 11-6mm. Go up one side and down the other. The bottom one is cut up the side facing the inside of the crest to the round end in the center. The other 11-6mm cut is on the outside of the frame going to the other round end which touches the shell. Then, to make the finish scroll lines in the round ends, you use push cuts with the 5-6mm and the 3-4mm to fit.

Fig. 6.44: Here I show how I shape the top of the lily leaves with a 5-12mm. I tilt the tool so one side of the leaf is higher than the other.

Fig. 6.45: With a 2 1/2 or 3-20mm and smaller sizes to fit, I clean up the background right down to the side mark of the center of the wood. I remove the wood with a 7-20mm or 12mm and will now smooth the background with the flatter tools.

Fig. 6.46: I cut downward with an 11-4mm to get the lily leaf tip to fold over its blade.

Fig. 6.47: Now, I shape the lily leaves with a 5-12mm. You do not have to cut to the full depth on the first cut. I cut off 2 to 4 mm at a time for better control. Here, I tilt the tool and push the blade to the background. I want one side to tilt down almost to the background while I keep the other side high. This cut assures a clean cut to the background. Then, I will undercut the back of this lily leaf with an 11-4mm.

Fig. 6.48: I use the V-tool to make the area between the lily leaves and the background a clean transition.

I am not going to go through the entire process on how to carve the lily leaves here. Carving the leaves was one of the projects to carve before carving this frame. If you made a paper model of the leaves and how they bend, you can use it now to see what you need to do. As you know, I use the 11-4mm to shape the leaf tips. One leaf tip curls over, so I cut at one angle. The other leaf tip curls under, so I make the opposite cut on the leaf tip below this and stop before I hit the leaf top. Both leaves are tilted and so are the tips. On the other side of the carving, the leaves are mirror images of these. I use the 5-12mm for the leaf tops. This is covered in detail in the "The Lily Leaves" carving section.

Fig. 6.49: Now, I start to work on the medallion, which is right between the two bottom scrolls. I shape the pearl with the inside of the 3-4mm tool.

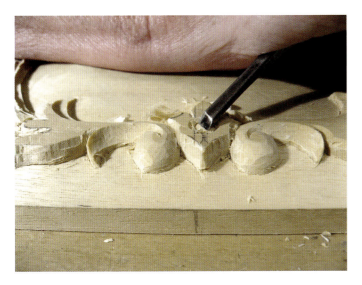

Fig. 6.50: I am shaping the pearl in the center of the medallion by push cutting with the 3-4mm.

Fig. 6.51: I cut the sides with a 3-12mm to get a little more shadow from it. You could also use a flat tool.

Fig. 6.52: The scrolls on the bottom of the crest flow back and into acanthus leaves. I cut the two deep concaves (one on the top side and one going into the scroll) with an 11-6mm. Then, I continue into the round head of the scroll with a 5-6mm and a 3-4mm to fit. Now, I am drawing in the lines from the pattern of the acanthus leaf. Then, I cut along the lines with an 11-4mm. You can see the finished center rosette in Fig. 6.52, and I'll just bet you can tell what tools were used. I used the 9-12mm (or similar deep gouge) for the top and sides, a 3-12mm (or flat tool) for the bottom sides, and an 11-2mm for the veins cut into the deep portion. By this point, I'll bet you could have carved the medallion without any help from me.

You can see the veins I cut in the shell with the 11-4mm and 2mm as described in Fig. 6.39. Look how beautifully this piece has cleaned up. What a wonderful crest! Congratulations, you now have a beautiful piece of European woodcarving to show off your newfound talents!

Now, we begin to carve the letters on the curved surface on the center of the Crest. You will need to know letter carving rather well. Before you begin to put any letters on your beautifully carved Crest, make sure you have done the letter carving chapter of this book until you are quite comfortable in the art of carving incised letters.

You should have a very good idea of how all the parts come together and have an excellent carving in front of you to prove it. Congratulations! However, if you are not happy with the results, this would be a great time to start another. You have every part fresh in your mind and should be able to go right through it. Just think of the first one as practice and a good learning experience. Now is the time to conquer the Crest.

If you have been carving part-time, don't get discouraged. You can see your progress, and you are getting excellent practice, so keep up the good work and before you know it, the Crest will be yours.

Fig. 6.53: Here is a good view of how I undercut the U that runs up each side of the crest pillow (or the inside of the crest) using a 7-6mm to fit. It stands proud and looks sharp.

Fig. 6.54: The letters are carefully transferred to the center of the Crest with the full size patterns taped in place and a piece of carbon paper slid underneath. Then, just follow the pattern lines with an ink pen. I put the letters H and L on my crest in honor of my father, Han Leereveld. He was a very famous Dutch carver. I remember when he was in his mid-'90s when I asked him if I could have his tools. He said, "No, no, you never know when a carving job will come along". With this fancy script, the letters look like R and L. I'm not concerned because every time I look at this Crest I think of him. I will reference my favorite letter book but for now, let's carve.

Fig. 6.55: I carefully remove the wood inside the lines of the letters. You will need tools that are extra sharp. I use a 39-10mm V-tool and a mallet to make the cuts right through the center of the lines.

Fig. 6.56: As I cut through the middle of the letters, I use everything I learned about incised letter carving. I am working on wood that is higher in the middle than it is at the sides. It's pillow-shaped. So, I must be careful to cut downhill.

Fig. 6.57: If the curve of the letter is very tight, I must cut shallow at first so as not to break any of the wood out.

Fig. 6.58: I have carved out the center of the letters with my 39-10mm V-tool. Notice that I did not finish some of the ends of the letters. I do them with other tools as you know from the letter carving chapter.

Fig. 6.59: Now, I widen the letter by taking the tool that best fits the curve. You can prepare for this when laying out the letter to be carved. If you have a 6 sweep, you can modify the letter a little to fit your 6 sweep. If all you have is a 5 sweep, then modify the drawing to fit your 5 sweep. This can pull the letter too far out of shape. If so, then use the letter as it is. Carve the curves with the tool that fits the curve the best. You can also use just part of the blade of your tool to make the cut whether the tool is a 5 or 6 or even a 7 sweep. Here I cut on an angle from the line on the wood to the middle V cut at the bottom. I use the tool that best fits this curve whether using the inside or outside of the tool. The convex curve here requires the inside of the tool to do the cutting.

Fig. 6.60: Here the best tool that fits that curve can cut like usual because the curve is concave. Again, I make push cuts, cutting at an angle from the pencil line to the middle of the bottom that was first established with my V-tool.

102

Fig. 6.61: I finish the sides of the letters with a 3-12mm held sideways. One side of the blade is in the V groove, and the rest of the blade sits right on the side of the letter. Next, we push the tool forward, following the side back to the pencil line. Cut a perfectly smooth side from the V groove on the bottom and the pencil line on the top. Slide the tool back and forth, keeping it in place. This gives an incredibly smooth side, burnished by the tool and with a slight indent from the 3 sweep that gives the letter a bit more shadow that really makes it stand out. I always finish up with a narrower V-tool, a 41-8mm or 10mm, to clean up the bottom of the letter. I carved out the ends of the letters with round dots with an 11-4mm.

Fig. 6.62: Here is a photo of the finished carving, letters and all.

You have probably noticed in some of these photos that the background was not perfectly smooth. Finish it off with a 3-20 or a 2 1/2 -20mm and smaller to fit. You start with the largest tool you have and work all the way down to the 3-4mm to reach in the tightest areas. You have a pillow-shaped surface inside the frame and a flat surface outside the frame. Make sure the background shows the hand tool cuts. They should show up very slightly, but it should not look like a sanded surface. The carving has to look like what it is, a hand-carved piece of art.

Fig. 6.63: I picked out a particular letter form from my favorite lettering book.

Fig. 6.64: The Book is Dover's "Gothic and Old English Alphabets" Selected and Arranged by Dan X. Solo. ISBN# 0-486-24695-7

Fig. 6.65: To finish up, go over the carving with 220 grit sandpaper just to take off any loose fibers on the edges, the fussy areas, not the hand-carved areas. Again, this is a hand-carved woodcarving, and we don't want to over sand.
The finish: First, I seal the entire panel with clear Watco and let it dry for a few days.

Fig. 6.66: Make sure you don't allow any pools of clear Watco oil to form. Brush them out of the tiny crevasses. After waiting a few days for the Watco oil to dry, continue by applying clear Briwax with a toothbrush and a soft cloth. Wait fifteen minutes and then buff it with a hard natural bristle brush to a deep beautiful shine. Then, apply light brown Briwax the same way over the whole panel and brush it off with a hard natural bristle brush. The entire finishing process is described at the end of Chapter 4 – "Seventeenth Century Dutch Panel".

Fig. 6.67: Your panel is now all sealed and with much more contrast due to the Briwax.

Congratulations On Your New Masterpiece!

Chapter 7
Some Passing Thoughts

From the very beginning of this book, I told you that I hoped you would experience the joy and thrill that I get every day when I walk into my studio to carve wood. I truly hope you have carved your way through this book and have enjoyed every carving in it. I hope that I have helped you to become a better woodcarver.

I took you through some challenging and exciting projects that included letter carving the old-fashioned way. Now you know that you don't need a room full of tools to carve wood. You just need a few well-chosen tools. To become a great woodcarver, all you need are the tools, good wood, and the desire to create.

I am sure that when many of you saw that "letter carving is not that complicated," you thought that goes against everything else you have read. When you saw the carving of a Seventeenth Century Dutch Panel you may have thought, "This is going to be fun? That is just too complex." When you saw the Crest you had to think, "How can I ever carve something with so many changing surfaces and then put my initials on a curved surface?" However, to those of you who took on these tasks, those of you who followed this book from the beginning to the end, I'll bet you now believe all those statements. You can look at a complex carving and take it on without intimidation, without a room full of tools. You know exactly what you need to create your own version of any complex carving.

As you carved, I said over and over, "Look at how my hands are", and "See how I hold this tool". If I said it once, I said it a hundred times, "See how I keep my wrist down so I have total control over the cutting edge". I used repetition to teach you how to carve. I said things over and over and over again. Why? If you followed and carved using this book from page 1 to the end, then you have a small idea of what it is like to have a master carver standing over you, constantly correcting and constantly watching. The old European masters that take in one or two apprentices are gone.

I was taught by an old European master, so I know what it is like to carve under one. The master kept a watchful eye. I still hear, "Now keep your wrist on the wood, and make sure your V-tool is right on the line. You don't want to make the carving larger than the pattern". Repetition is an effective way to teach.

The way I taught you to carve was like the way I learned to carve. I became your master; you became my student. You may have thought, "Too much". But you can look at any carving and instead of thinking, "That's too complicated", you know the process for how to do that carving by heart. You know what tool you will use first and how to proceed from there. You have become a competent woodcarver, and, with practice, will possibly become a master. I wish you happy carving!

Appendix A

I've provided this guide to identify the shape of the various tools that I have talked about in this book. These are the tools that I use the most. Please note that this guide is not meant to be a comprehensive list of carving tools.

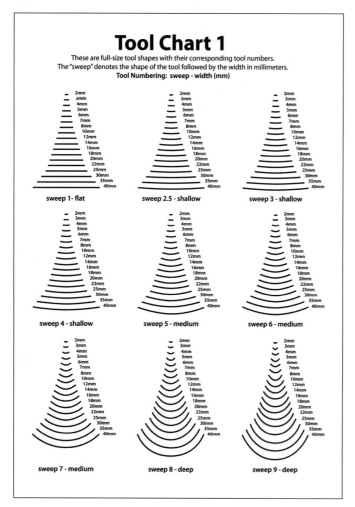

Enlarge drawing 225% for correct tool cross sections

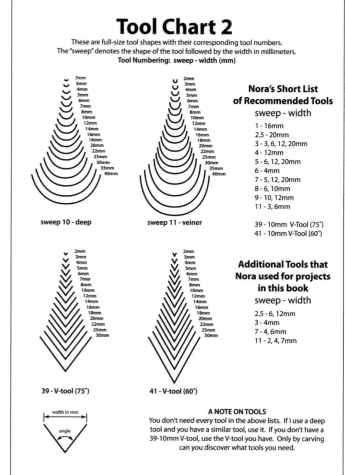

Enlarge drawing 225% for correct tool cross sections

Appendix B

See www.norahall.com for copies of Nora Hall's instructional woodcarving DVDs, study casts, woodcarving packages, carving patterns, and more.

Nora Hall's Sample Portfolio

This 6'-6" high English style mantle was carved from black walnut. The home is located in Red Mountain Aspen, Colorado.

Scroll design corbel with free flowing leaves

Free flowing branch detail at the center of mantel frieze

Full size clay model of corbel for client's approval

This 9'-4" high lion design fireplace mantel was carved in white oak. The home is located in Denver, Colorado.

Finished parts of the walnut mantel prior to mounting in the home (2 corbels & frieze)

Test mounting the mantel corbel

These six-foot high Oriental style dragons were carved in bass wood. The columns were placed on either side of a raised fireplace hearth and were capped with capitals that met the ceiling.

This six-foot high Oriental style panel was carved in teak.

This detail shows the lifelike reproductions of the animals.

These 14" corbels were carved in Virginia white oak.

These dual bi-fold doors were carved in mahogany. They are located in a sanctuary of a synagogue in Denver, Colorado. The height of the tree is 12 feet. The overall height of the archway is 16 feet.

This is one of six panels I carved that were inspired by Alphonse Mucha's drawings. These panels are over five feet high and were carved in sugar pine.

This teak wood wall hanging is about four feet wide and carved in the style of Grinling Gibbons.

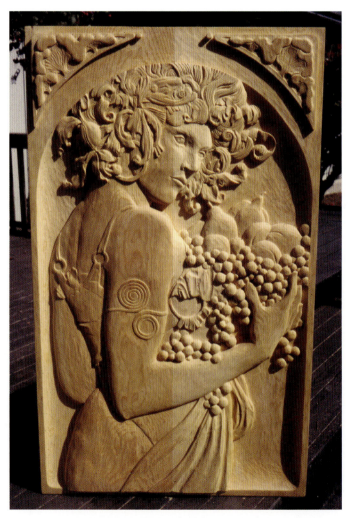

Another one of the six Alphonse Mucha's inspired panels.

Appendix B - Letters L & S
Reduce or enlarge to suit your needs.

Permission is granted to make a limited number of copies of this pattern for personal use only.

Appendix B - Letters B & J
Reduce or enlarge to suit your needs.

Permission is granted to make a limited number of copies of this pattern for personal use only.

Appendix B - Crest
Crest Details

Reduce or enlarge to suit your needs.

Permission is granted to make a limited number of copies of this pattern for personal use only.

Appendix B - Seventeenth Century Dutch Panel
Linenfold Detail

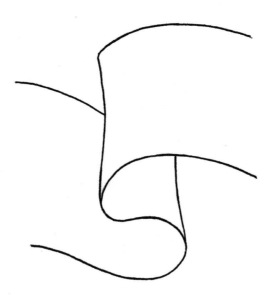

Permission is granted to make a limited number of copies of this pattern for personal use only.